JESUS UNBRANDED

VOLUME 2

STORIES WITH BITE

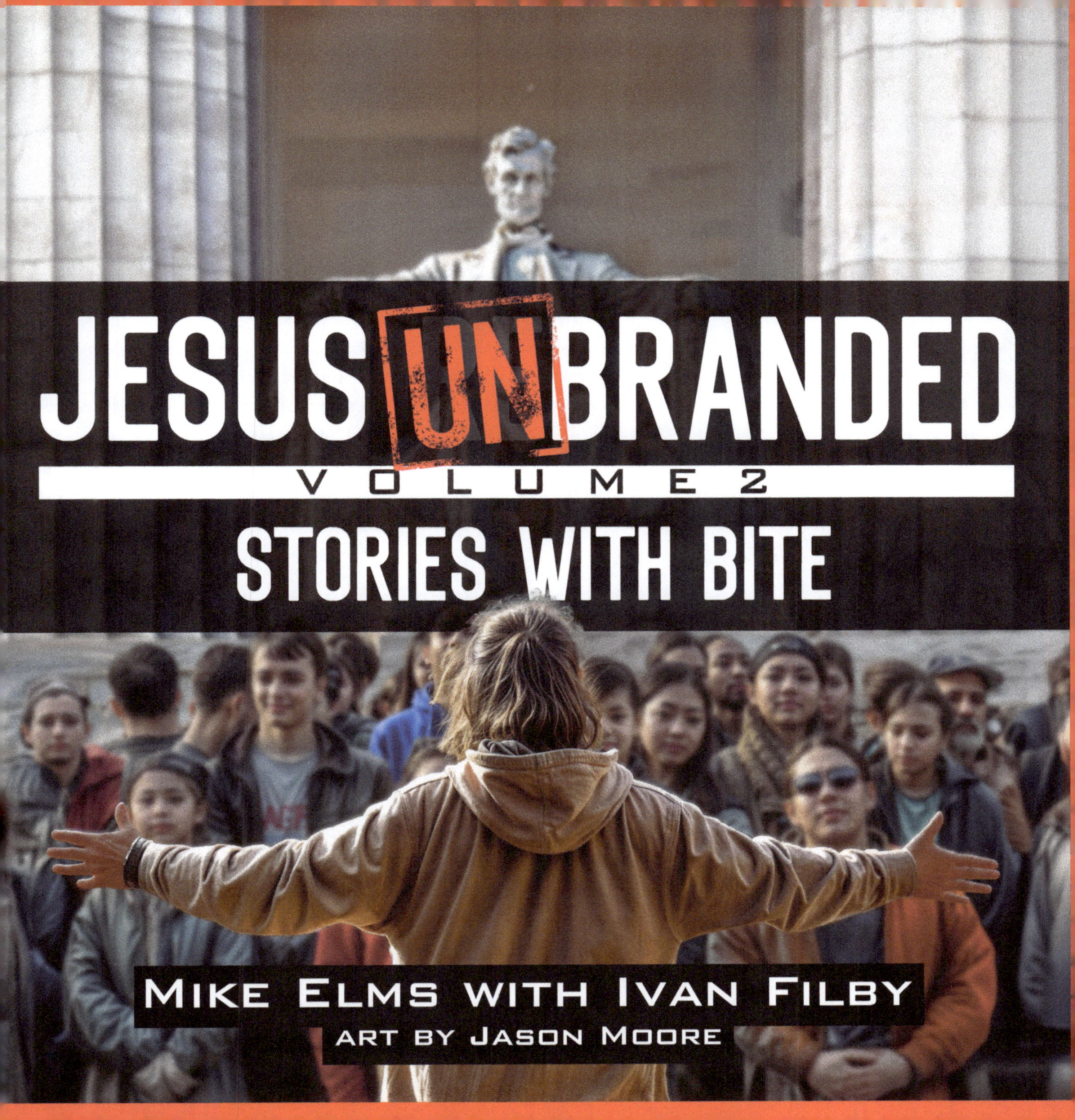

JESUS UN BRANDED
VOLUME 2
STORIES WITH BITE

MIKE ELMS WITH IVAN FILBY

ART BY JASON MOORE

Jesus Unbranded: Volume Two
Stories With Bite

Copyright 2025 by Mike Elms, Ivan Filby, and Jason Moore

This book is printed on acid-free, elemental chlorine-free paper.

978-1-963265-32-3

All scripture quotations are taken from THE HOLY BIBLE, NEW INTERNATIONAL VERSION®, NIV® Copyright © 1973, 1978, 1984, 2011 by Biblica, Inc.™ Used by permission of Zondervan. All rights reserved worldwide.

24 25 26 27 28 29 30 31 32 33—10 9 8 7 6 5 4 3 2 1

MANUFACTURED in the UNITED STATES of AMERICA

Contents

Also available

Jesus unbranded: volume one
Stories without spin

. . . .

The parables

Listen up
- When new into old won't go
- The farewell tour and the Ferrari
- The astute and reckless investors
- The two punters
- The selfish lawyer
- The night watch
- The CEO's dilemma
- The failing project
- The reluctant advertiser.

Listening up

Heaven is...
- Junk mail
- The retirement fund
- Look up and look in
- The nickel and the carp
- The job applications
- The wine merchant

...Heaven is

Mark my words
- The two drivers
- The vindictive landlord
- The caring Russian Ultra
- The panicking colleague

- A dramatic night at the Oscars
- The free lunch
- The no-good do-gooders

Marked by his words

It was a Sunday in Meopham, a small village in southeast England, an hour's drive from London.

The autumnal sunshine was lancing through the windows of the small Baptist chapel.

Dust motes pirouetted in the sunbeams as the Pastor read Matthew 22:1-14: The Parable of the Wedding Banquet.

I looked at the faces around me and saw many blank expressions.

A number had closed eyes, but closed in vexation, rather than meditation.

Some younger eyes were downcast.

Cast downwards onto their mobile phone.

But onto YouTube, rather than YouVersion.

All the signs of a disengaged congregation.

The Pastor finished the reading and picked up the notes of his sermon.

I thought to myself: *"Your congregation has lost interest before you've even started."*

I recalled that this parable was the final part of a trilogy of parables Jesus told during Holy Week. It followed hard on the heels of the parables of the Tenants and the Two Sons.

All three were told in public spaces. Together, they formed a scathing attack on the religious authorities in Jerusalem. Their meaning to the authorities and the crowd would have been clear. The authorities would have been furious, the crowd delighted.

One thing was for sure. No one there would have been disengaged or disinterested.

Jesus never, ever, bored people.

And then I thought: *Guinness.*

At that time, I was CEO of a big ad agency in London with a long list of blue-chip clients including Ford, American Express, Unilever, Shell, Nestlé, Microsoft, and Reebok.

And Guinness, which in Adland, is iconic. The brand had been built upon several decades worth of cutting-edge advertising, but those ads had failed to move with the times and were now failing to enthuse its consumers.

While a brand can survive many things, it cannot survive irrelevance and indifference.

So, Guinness was in poor shape. Marginalized. Struggling.

Our challenge was to put the sparkle back into its ads, to put Guinness back on its prestigious advertising pedestal. And, by so doing, to connect the brand with a whole new audience.

We did so by casting Rutger Hauer as "The Man with the Guinness," who ruminated on life, the universe, and everything, underscored by the tagline, "Guinness, Pure Genius."

The campaign was idiosyncratic, bemusing, challenging.

It was applauded by some and derided by others.

It intrigued some and baffled others.

What people were not was disinterested. What the ads were not, was ignored. The campaign created interest and debate. It got people talking.

It didn't change the brand. It took it back to its roots. Re-affirmed it. Revitalized it.

(At that time, our family lived in an Edwardian country house. When first built in 1901 it was at the cutting edge of technology. It had electricity! But 100 years later, the electrical system was obsolete. So, we had it rewired. The house was once again fit for purpose.)

Guinness was back center stage. Rewired. Once again fit for purpose.

Today the brand name alone is valued at over $2 billion dollars.

The essence of great advertising is that it is cutting-edge.

It has to cut through. To cut through media noise, and to cut into people's minds.

"Just do it!"

"Finger Lickin' Good"

"Where's the beef?"

"Don't leave home without it!"

Catch my drift? (Not an ad campaign, but it could be!)

The parables Jesus told had real "cut-through."

He knew his audiences, he knew the culture, he knew the messaging he wanted to convey, and he constructed his storylines accordingly.

Some entertained, some shocked, some challenged, some affirmed.

But all connected with their audiences and conveyed the underlying messaging that Jesus wanted to get across.

Jesus never, ever, bored people.

Finally, I thought: *Jesus may have been a carpenter, but he'd have also made a great adman!*

I recalled that I was taught in my earliest days as an adman that the golden rule in advertising is to stand in the shoes of your audience, to see things from their perspective and communicate accordingly.

I think maybe that's one of the reasons why Jesus came to us, as one of us.

As the Pastor started unpacking the parable, I sat back to try to concentrate.

However, yet another thought came to mind. But this one wasn't my thought. Unbidden, this one was livestreamed into my brain:

Mike, the culture of your society, here and today, is very different from the one I preached into 2000 years ago. The stories I told then don't connect and resonate in the same way now.

I could see that by looking at the faces around me. Storylines woven around Samaritans, virgins with lamps, fig trees, Pharisees, vineyards, and three thousand litres of olive oil don't have the sort of impact now as they had when first told in first-century Palestine.

Mike, use your skills to create new storylines that will refresh the Parables brand. Tell them the way you think I'd tell them, here and now. Stand in my shoes, as I stand in their shoes. Keep the messaging the same but make the stories relevant. Give them cut-through. Make them fit for purpose. Rewire them!

I balked at this: "Lord, I'm not a theologian, I'm an adman."

Mike, that's exactly why I'm giving this task to you.

As a committed Christian and as a seasoned adman, I knew I had been given a Mission:
"Keep my stories alive."

Then God sent Ivan my way, a man full of the Spirit and theology and keen to join with me on that Mission. And so we set to work.

And then he sent Jason to join us. Very Trinitarian!

Mike Elms
London, 2024

Wired | Stories that carry power

Most of us can recall an outstanding teacher
from our schooldays:

par·a·ble(s)
an earthly story
with a spiritual truth

- A teacher with a passion for their subject and for us.

- A teacher with great wisdom.

- A teacher with a unique teaching style.

- A teacher that made us want to learn.

- A teacher that left an indelible mark on our lives.

Jesus was all this and more.

- A brilliant teacher who also happened to be the Son of God.

- A teacher in whom two worlds intersected, the spiritual and the physical, heaven and earth.

- At the heart of his teaching lie the parables.

- Stories that he created and related in his own words.

- Stories that he told to reconcile his two perspectives.

- Stories that use familiar, everyday settings to convey eternal, spiritual themes.

- Stories that we can understand and from which we can learn life-changing truths.

To spend time with the parables is to spend time with Jesus, with his disciples, with the crowds that followed him, and even with the authorities that opposed him.

To spend time with the parables enables us to see and engage with the spiritual themes that permeate the events, relationships, and situations in our everyday lives.

The lives that we are living, here and today.

Rewired | When is a tablet not a tablet?

Jesus was passionate about getting his message across.

We can see his frustration as even his closest followers struggled to get it:

You of little faith, why are you talking among yourselves about having no bread? Do you still not understand.... How is it you don't understand that I was not talking to you about bread? (Matthew 16: 8,9,11)

To remedy their lack of understanding, Jesus used props and storylines drawn from everyday life.

Things that were culturally relevant.

Stories that true faith-seekers could understand and relate to.

This begs a question: If Jesus were telling these stories to us today, here and now, would he not realize that we are unfamiliar with the way of life of a first-century, middle eastern agricultural society?

Of course, he would. So, surely, he would create and relate stories rooted in the 21st-century?

In the Americas, Europe, Asia, Africa, Oceania, he'd find similar cultural touchpoints, so keen is he that all grasp his message and have an opportunity to respond to his claims.

He would draw upon modern-day commerce, entertainment, media, technology, sports, medicine, and social protocols, and he would use them as physical, everyday analogies and storylines to communicate his eternal, spiritual themes.

He would keep the themes and messaging of the stories unchanged.

But he would wire his words into today's world.

This thought first struck Mike in the closing years of the last century. It gave birth to the rewiring of the "Good Samaritan" as the *"Compassionate Millwall fan."* (In the United Kingdom, fans of the Millwall soccer team are not noted for their sociability, gentleness of disposition, or considerate behavior towards others![1])

· ·

[1]Perhaps like a Philadelphia Eagles fan today.—The Publisher (who is also a Dallas Cowboys fan).

One Sunday he preached on it.

People told him that it worked well, and they encouraged him to write more.

So, he did. This led him to write a short sermon series, after which, he could feel God nudging him to write still more. Eventually, he realized he was being nudged to rewire all of the parables.

At first, Mike resisted the nudge. He didn't have the time. He had too many marketing consultancy projects. He had a family, and he was training for marathons.

Plus, it felt like an intimidating challenge. Jesus told a lot of parables.

But the nudge became an increasingly more forceful shove.

God simply shut down his marketing projects.

Mike and his wife, Valerie, became empty nesters.

He soon realized that he would not better his 3h 43m marathon in Chicago.

Eventually, he capitulated and sat down at his keyboard.

Closed his eyes and prayed.

Opened his spirit and wrote.

Then Ivan joined the party.

Ivan met Mike at an event at the House of Lords. They chatted about their writing projects, and Mike handed Ivan a copy of *Parables: Rewired* in a brown paper envelope! Rightly so: Jesus' parables are dangerous stuff.

Ivan read them all in one sitting at Heathrow Airport and laughed out loud.

Then, he read them again, one by one, in many sittings.

One day in a phone conversation, Ivan threw out the challenge: "Mike, you need to rewire your book of parables for our friends in North America. I can help if you like."

Mike liked. And so, the Good Samaritan became the "Caring Russian Ultra," and together we developed a method of working.

Our first task was to identify the main message Jesus sought to communicate.

That had to be respected and protected at all costs.

We've submitted our work to eminent theologians to check that we have achieved this. They say we have. We pray that they are right.

The parables often contain sub-themes, which we suspect were not Jesus' main thrust or even intent, but which, as so often is the case in storytelling, grew unbidden out of the storyline. We set out to identify these and, where possible, bring them out in our rewiring.

We think we've been reasonably successful but not universally so. Sometimes it has proved impossible to replicate all of the first-century cultural analogies entirely.

On the other hand, some sub-themes have emerged from our own storytelling. Where we are conscious that this is the case, we have checked them against Jesus' teaching. If they have stood scrutiny, we have let them remain.

For instance, you'll see that we have used a ski slope white-out in our rewiring of the Lost Sheep. When Mike preached on the story, a keen skier in the congregation said the concept transfixed her. In a white-out, she said, you feel isolated, afraid, and terribly alone. The retelling had helped her see the parable from the sheep's perspective, lost in a spiritual white-out.

We had not spotted this, and it's entirely likely that there are other sub-messages that we have not spotted. As you read these stories, they may speak a message peculiar to you and to you alone. If so, listen hard, because it's not from us: it's God speaking directly to you.

Finally, and crucially, we must stress that we have rewired the parables to supplement the originals, not to replace them, which is why we have also included the stories as Jesus himself told them.

We happily acknowledge that Jesus was a far better storyteller than we are!

This is a resource book.

When you read it make sure you have a pen in your hand and use it, liberally.

Cross out what you don't agree with. Underline what you do.

Amend. Annotate.

Don't feel a need to read the whole book in one go. Take your time. Take as much time to read it as it has taken us to write it. Hint: that's a lot of time. As you read, have a cup of tea or coffee. Read it by yourself. Then maybe discuss it over a meal with some friends. That's very biblical and exactly what the original hearers may have done.

Each parable follows the same format:

Rewiring

As we've said, the themes and messaging of the parables are timeless, but the storylines are time limited. The product is terrific, but the packaging is perhaps a little dated. Imagine a world without teabags or without squeezable honey and mayonnaise, a world of hard un-spreadable butter, milk only in glass bottles. You might be saying: "Oh, yes please," in which case you may like this next part.

Reminding

After each 'rewiring', we've included the original parable. It's in the NIV translation. Sorry if that's not your bag. There's always Bible Gateway!

Resetting and retelling happen a lot. Think about Joe Cocker's cover of the Beatles' *With a Little Help from My Friends* or the remake of *The Italian Job*.

On just about every episode of *America's Got Talent* or *The Voice*, you'll hear new interpretations of old classics.

And, shocker, Bradley Cooper's and Lady Gaga's 2018 movie, *A Star is Born*, is also a remake of the 1954 release, itself a reinterpretation of the original release from 1937.

People retell stories, remake movies, or rerecord songs to keep them relevant and alive.

We're both Shakespeare junkies. Consequently, we've seen many productions that reset his plays in a modern setting. Often, they add fresh angles, which expand and enrich our experience. But invariably, we find ourselves cross-referring back to the original text. It's great to hold the two in tension.

That's another reason why we've included the original parables.

Interpretation

Occasionally the Gospels show Jesus having to explain his parables to his audience. Given that the audience who didn't get it often included the people who wrote or inspired the Gospels, we suspect that Jesus had to explain his stories more times than they cared to record!

This knowledge brought us to the tricky bit.

Our original intention was to just rewire the stories and let the audience take it from there. But our friends urged us not to do that. They said it would be a complete cop-out. They pushed us to draw out some messaging and implications, and 'hotwire' them to us, here and now.

Mike's an adman, not an ordained clergyman and does not have a degree in theology. But as an ad man, Mike knows how to get a message across. This has equipped him to become an experienced preacher.

Ivan however is an ordained minister with deep theological insight. He also has a ton of training in business. This has equipped him to become an experienced professor, dean, and university president.

Together, we've found, we make a great team.

Even so, look on our 'hotwiring thoughts' as a starter for ten. If they are helpful, great—build on them. If they're not, please feel free to ignore them.

But, either way, do take time to think about what the parable (original, rewired, or we strongly suggest, the two together) may be saying to you here and now.

Reflection

Jesus was the consummate teacher. When he wasn't telling stories, he was asking questions.

We like both approaches.

So, we've also posed some questions which we've had the temerity to upgrade and call "Reflections."

Response

This section is always blank, as we have nothing to say here, because this is all about you. What you think and say is as important as anything we've written in this book.

As authors, we know how intimidating a blank section can be. But we encourage you to try and write something, anything.

Look at it as a letter to Jesus.

That's what we did and look at where it has led us.

Where to start

Many authors say that the first page is the most difficult, that their brain suddenly becomes as blank as the page or screen.

But that's about *how* to start, and that wasn't our problem.

We were presented with umpteen parables. Potential storylines were firing our brains, not freezing them.

No, our problem was *where* to start. Which parable should be first, and what should be the order thereafter?

In our first draft, we decided to take things in biblical order: start with the parables recorded by Matthew, then onto Mark, and finally sweep up with Luke. (John wasn't big on parables!) Then we were struck by a Big Idea. How about putting them into chronological order?

Great idea.

Bad idea.

We rapidly discovered that biblical chronology is fraught with challenges. We knew that was the case with the Old Testament, but surely the New Testament would be a lot easier, particularly the Gospels. Nope. For instance, we discovered that John's Gospel is the only one that makes it clear that Jesus' ministry spanned three years. Matthew, Mark, and Luke were more concerned with recording what happened, rather than when and in what order.

So, there are mismatches within and across the Gospels. Theologians of infinitely greater eminence than we have helpfully put forward varying suggestions on sequencing, which then, unhelpfully, differ.

It became clear to us that coming up with a chronology of Jesus' ministry and then inserting the parables within that was the theological equivalent of the search for the Holy Grail. Like Lancelot and Indiana Jones, we persevered. Our research offered several interpretations. All we had to do was choose one. But which one?

One, in particular, stood out, because it listed the first parable to be told as new wine into old wineskins and the last as sheep and goats. This meant that Jesus' first parable was about wine and told at the same time as his first miracle at the wedding in Cana, which was also all about wine. Both the parable and the miracle presaged the beginning of his ministry. That worked for us. It also meant that his last parable was about his second coming and Judgement Day. That also worked for us.

In fact, we became incredibly excited because we were seeing the parables in a new way: in the light of Jesus' ministry.

Chronology

Timeline of Jesus' Ministry	Timeline of the Parables
AD 26	
Summer • Baptism	
• Wilderness temptations	
Autumn • First miracle: water into wine	1 • New cloth and new wine
AD 27	
Winter • Cleansing of the Temple	
Summer • Andrew, Peter, James and John join	
Autumn • Matthew joins	
AD 28	
Winter • Jesus chooses the 12 disciples	
• Woman at the well	
Spring • Sermon on the Mount	2-3 • Lamp under bushel > wise and foolish builders
Summer • Travel through Galilee	4-9 • Debtors and creditor > sower
Autumn • Calming the storm; disciples sent out	10-17 • 'Heaven is' series
AD 29	
Winter • Feeding of the 5000	
Spring • Walks on water	
Summer • Transfiguration	18-19 • Master and servant > unmerciful servant
Autumn • Raising of Lazarus	20-21 • Good Samaritan > Friend in need
AD 30	
Winter • Journey to Jerusalem	22-24 • Places of honour > counting the cost
• Healing of blind Bartimaeus	25-33 • 'Lost and found' series; shrewd steward > talents
Spring • Visit to Martha and Mary	
• Palm Sunday	
• Cleansing of the Temple	34-36 • *Meek, mild, as if* series
• Last Supper, arrest and crucifixion	37-39 • *Where do you stand?* series
• Resurrection	

Stories with bite

We decided to publish this book as two volumes for two reasons.

The first was practical.

There are, in total, 39 different parables recorded across the Gospels of Matthew, Mark and Luke. We decided to create a couple of 'combi-parables', but that still left 37. By the time we had rewired them, included the originals, added a commentary and reflection, left space and time for reader input, and then added art; we realized we were looking at a very large book! Too large.

The second reason was spiritual.

You'll see that our chronology has Jesus telling parables in a ministry that lasted a little over three years. (That matches what most historians believe, although there are some who would contend it was just one year. But, hey, this is our book and we're going to side with the majority!)

Once we had placed all the parables in the context of Jesus' ministry, we could see very clearly that they divided into two types with two different purposes.

Jesus spent most of the first three years of his ministry travelling around Galilee and surrounding areas, (including brief visits to Jerusalem, depending on how one interprets the various and varying Gospel timelines).

The tone of the parables he told was engaging, surprising, sometimes light-hearted, other times shocking, and always illuminating.

These were *'teaching parables'*.

'Stories without spin'.

Then, late in the third year, the winter of AD 29/30 Jesus 'set his face' toward Jerusalem and the climax of his ministry.

The tone of the parables he told during this period was massively different. They were urgent, darker, and politically super-charged.

These were *'preaching parables'*.

'Stories with bite'.

The first volume, *Jesus Unbranded: Stories Without Spin*, focused on the teaching parables.

You don't need to have read that to appreciate this book.

So please do read on.

But when you reach the end of this book, we urge you to get your hands on Volume One.

You'll then have the complete parables collection, the whole story of the stories.

This second volume, *Jesus Unbranded: Stories With Bite*, focuses upon the 'preaching parables' and traces the dramatic events leading up to and into Jesus' final journey to Jerusalem, during which he adopts a gloves-off approach to his story-telling. An approach which was to cost him his life.

We have grouped these into four series.

The first, *'Lost and Found,'* comprises just three parables. But what a trio they are. It is often said of Jesus that he came to seek the lost. The only flaw with that statement is that 'seek' is such an inadequate word.

If you have ever lost anything, or anyone, that means the world to you, you'll know how desperately you desired to find it, or them, again. To have it or her or him back. You'll know the depth of the sense of loss; the heartfelt yearning to salve it.

These stories are full of those raw emotions.

The second set of six stories were also told on the journey to Jerusalem.

We've called them *'Travelers Tales'* because we could imagine Jesus telling them late in the evening over a smouldering campfire. And then, after supper, he and the disciples discussing them, pulling them apart, interrogating them, getting to the core messaging.

They were Jesus' last coaching session. And the core messaging cut straight to the heart of the societal values of the day: religious and political. Stood them up, dissected them, tore them apart and then turned them on their head. A conflation of rock, jazz, jam and rap.

Be warned: none of them make for comfortable or easy reading. Make sure your brain is in gear!

And then, in the three-part series we've titled *'Meek, Mild, As If'* Jesus turned the volume control up to max.

A senior Anglican Bishop once said to Mike: too many people are happy to see the baby Jesus laying meek and mild in his manger—and leave him there.

These stories give both the truth and the lie to that notion. Too many people are happy to leave him there. But Jesus wasn't happy to stay there. Oh no. Far, far from it.

These stories see Jesus upping the ante in his attack on religious and political hypocrisy and mendacity.

They are stories that demand and deserve a reaction.

Then and now. Read them with respect.

Meek, Mild, As If!

And then we reach the final parables Jesus told.

Just three of them, which we've grouped together as a series titled *'Where Do You Stand?'*

By now Jesus knew his human fate was sealed. But also that his spiritual future lay before him in eternity. He believed that. He knew that. With a certainty to the power of infinity.

He knew that he was about to leave this world; but he also knew that he would return to it. To renew it. To re-create it.

So these final, three stories he told and the contingent questions he asked were binary. They left no opportunity, no room, for sitting on the fence.

Does our belief and certainty match his?

Where do you stand?

Jesus leaves it up to each of us as to how we answer.

The parables volume two | Stories with bite

Rewired	Original

Lost (and found)
The missing pupil · Lost sheep
The lost wedding ring · · · · · · · · · · · · · · · · · · Lost coin
The tale of the teenage wastrel · · · · · · · · · · · · Prodigal son
(Lost) and found

Travellers' tales
The sassy theme park manager · · · · · · · · · · · · Shrewd steward
The two landlords · Rich man and Lazarus
The laborers on the building site · · · · · · · · · · · Workers in the vineyard
The referee's tale · Persistent widow
Sparring on the stump · · · · · · · · · · · · · · · · · · Pharisee and the tax collector
The store managers · Talents
Travellers' tales told

Meek, mild, as if...
The two plumbers · Two sons
The rebellious board · · · · · · · · · · · · · · · · · · · Tenants
The big game · Wedding banquet
...Meek, mild, as if

Where do <u>you</u> stand?
Tales of the expected · · · · · · · · · · · · · · · · · · · Fig tree
The impatient paparazzi · · · · · · · · · · · · · · · · · Ten virgins
A shanty of sailboats and motorboats · · · · · · · · Sheep and goats
Where do <u>you</u> stand?

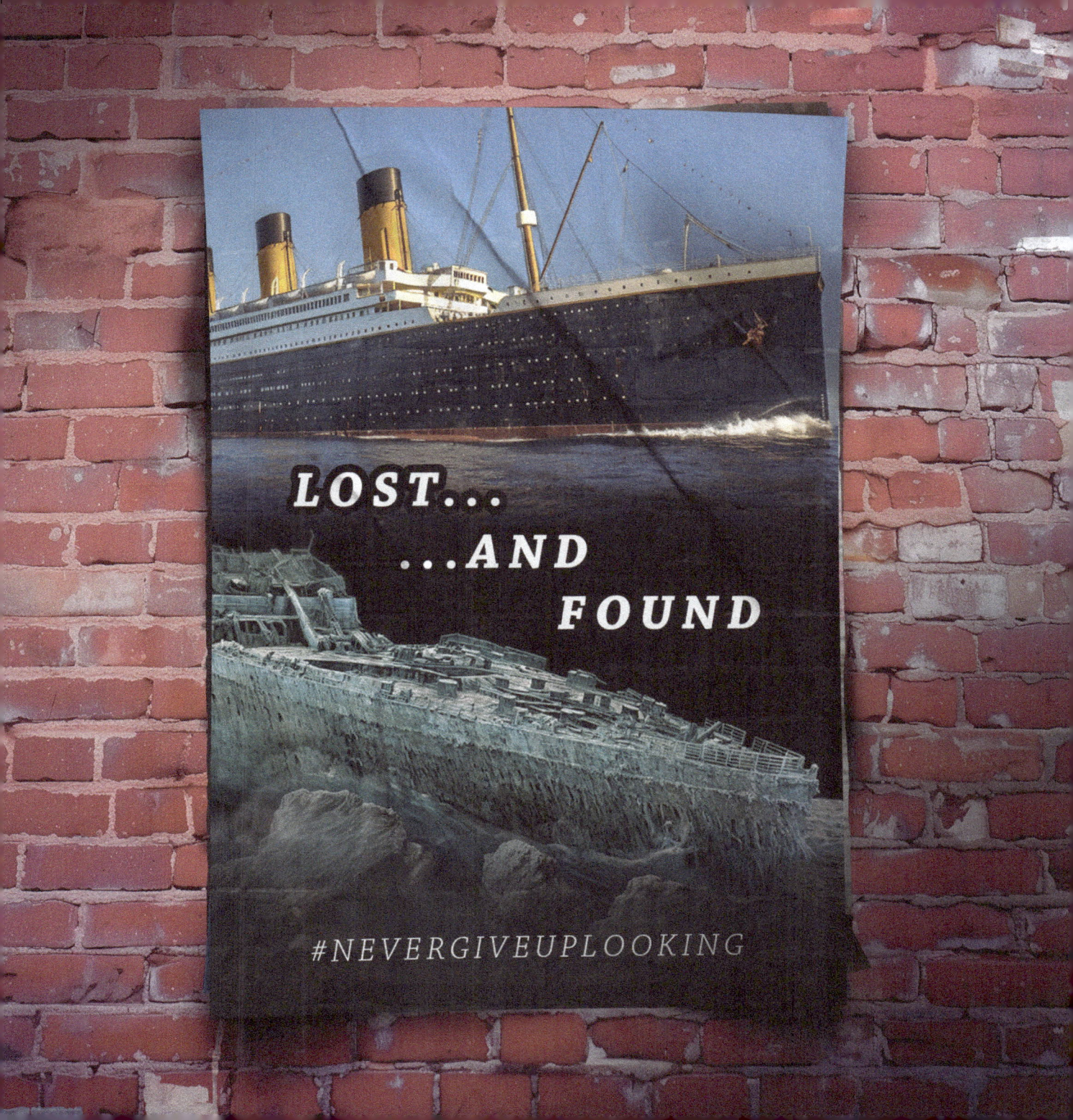

In Luke's Gospel (Chapter 15), Jesus recounts three consecutive stories about three things being lost: a sheep, a coin, and a son.

Each lost item is dearly loved and sadly missed by the person who lost it.

Each one of them is desperate, to the point of distraction, to find and recover their loss.

In each case, the lost item is subsequently found and returned to its rightful place, and the owner's sense of loss is replaced by great joy.

God the Father, God the Son, and God the Spirit are unceasingly, relentlessly and passionately seeking each and every one of their creation that they fear they may have lost.

It was clearly a message that Jesus wanted to reinforce so even people like Ivan and I would get the point.

Any time any one of us turns our face Heavenwards, there is a massive party thrown in Heaven to welcome us.

Party on!

THE MISSING PUPIL

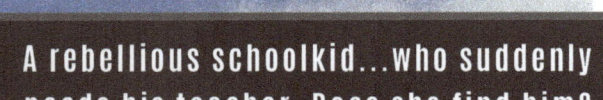

A rebellious schoolkid...who suddenly needs his teacher. Does she find him?

Jesus had been talking about the need for people to re-think faith issues. He wanted them to forgo the prevailing legalistic mindset and approach faith anew through the eyes of a child. To illustrate this, he told the famous parable of the shepherd and the lost sheep:

· ·

Ollie was tumbling in a white gyroscope.

Ollie the "Beast of Year 9."

Ollie was petrified.

Charlotte began the headcount.

Things had started so well.

The dawn of the ski trip on Mammoth Mountain had slowly drawn its curtains on a cloudless, deep blue sky and a sparkling white snowscape.

She and the other four teachers had shepherded the kids onto the ski-bus to the base of the mountain and then onto the 2,000-foot gondola ride to the ski slopes.

Where, after the dreaded ski-off assessment run, their 100 pupil charges had been split into five groups ranked by experience and ability, each group with a local ski instructor.

Ollie couldn't stop himself falling.

Ollie the "King of Detention."

Ollie gasped.

The first three groups were first-timers, and they were taken to the nursery slopes.

The fourth group had a couple of weeks' experience and headed off to the blue runs.

The remaining handful ventured further afield across the mountain to some stiff reds and blacks.

Charlotte, the trip leader and most experienced skier, patrolled the nursery slopes and the blue runs checking on the progress of her less experienced pupils.

Fun in the sun.

She promised herself that she would have even more fun showing her elite group the way down the black runs later in the week.

Then the weather turned.

Ollie saw his ski detach and disappear into the white.

Ollie the "Enforcer."

Ollie screamed.

The cloud base dropped like a doomed elevator. The bright blue sky became steely grey. A biting wind set in.

The fun disappeared.

Fortunately, the local ski instructors knew their mountain and had anticipated events. They knew it was time to get off the mountain.

Charlotte supervised the groups as they assembled at the top of the gondola.

As the three nursery groups started their descent back down, the fourth group was returning from their blue runs.

So far, so good. Ninety pupils on their way. The 10 black runners were higher up the mountain but should be back shortly.

Ollie felt his face numbing.

Ollie the "Teacher Tamer."

Ollie wept.

Charlotte counted in the elite group.

...7, 8, 9.

"Where's the tenth?" she yelled at the instructor.

He looked at her blankly.

"For goodness' sake," she said, heading for the nearest ski lift.

She reached the top. It was even worse than she had feared, a complete white-out, with visibility down to a couple of yards.

There were two slopes back down the mountain: Red 4 and Black 13. Reasoning that the instructor would have chosen the easier route, she headed off down Red 4.

Charlotte prayed.

Ollie felt so alone.

Ollie the infamous "One and Only."

Ollie prayed.

Charlotte saw a dark shape just ahead and to her left.

Instinctively she stabbed her right leg, her downward ski, into the slope to come to a juddering stop, downslope of Ollie.

She reached out and grabbed him.

"Take off your ski."

He looked at her. "For once in your life just do as you are told!"

Ollie did as he was told.

Charlotte grabbed him. "Stand on my skis in front of me."

That night 99 pupils were sipping hot chocolate and swapping stories of their great adventure.

But Charlotte was still hugging her 100th charge.

Who, for the first time in his life, was enjoying being the teacher's pet.

The parable of the lost sheep

Luke 15:3-7

Matthew 18:12-13

³Then Jesus told them this parable: ⁴"Suppose one of you has a hundred sheep and loses one of them. Doesn't he leave the ninety-nine in the open country and go after the lost sheep until he finds it? ⁵And when he finds it, he joyfully puts it on his shoulders ⁶and goes home. Then he calls his friends and neighbors together and says, 'Rejoice with me; I have found my lost sheep.' ⁷I tell you that in the same way there will be more rejoicing in heaven over one sinner who repents than over ninety-nine righteous persons who do not need to repent.

¹²"What do you think? If a man owns a hundred sheep, and one of them wanders away, will he not leave the ninety-nine on the hills and go to look for the one that wandered off? ¹³And if he finds it, truly I tell you, he is happier about that one sheep than about the ninety-nine that did not wander off.

So, what's this story saying to US, here and now?

We don't know about you, but we don't know many shepherds.

But we do know lots of teachers.

Mike's daughter, Charlotte, is one: a PE teacher. She leads ski trips. She was the inspiration for the rewiring of the parable.

We don't know a lot of lost sheep either.

But we do know a lot of lost people.

We all do. The world is full of lost souls.

You and we are unlikely to be able to reach them all.

(Although, with God on our side, we should be careful never to rule anything completely out.)

But this parable talks about a particular kind of lost sheep.

In his gospel, Matthew calls it a wandering sheep, one that was once part of the flock, secure in the fold, but is now absent.

According to research compiled by churchtrac.com, churches typically see a 10%-15% attrition rate every year.

In 2000, 32% of Americans attended church on a weekly basis. By 2023, that number had dropped to 20%. Pre-pandemic, approximately 3,500 people were leaving religious congregations every day. That's a total of 1.2 million people wandering away each year. In 2023, churches were at 85% of their pre-pandemic attendance level.

Many sheep have wandered and are yet to return.

How about your church? Has anyone stopped coming?

Maybe it has been a gradual process and they have simply dropped off the radar.

Maybe they dropped out because of the pandemic.

Maybe they were a bit of an Ollie.

Maybe this has been happening for years.

Maybe it's only now as you read this that you realise that you haven't seen someone for a while.

Maybe you could seek them out on social media, give them a call.

Or, better still, drop in to see them.

Reflection and prayer | Do I know any 'lost sheep'?

. . . .

_____

_____

_____

_____

_____

_____

What's this story saying to me, here and now?

. . . .

_____

_____

_____

_____

_____

THE LOST WEDDING RING

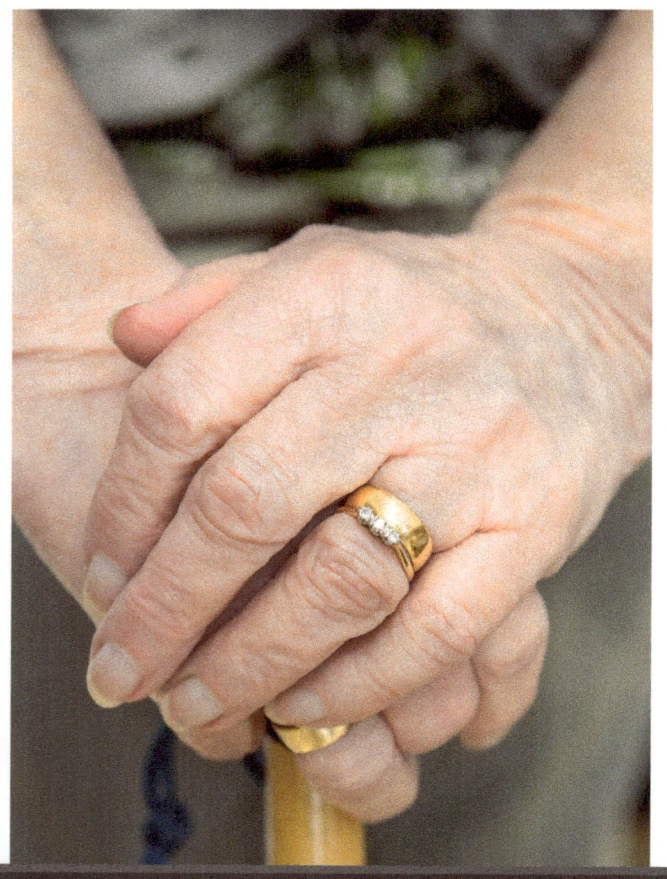

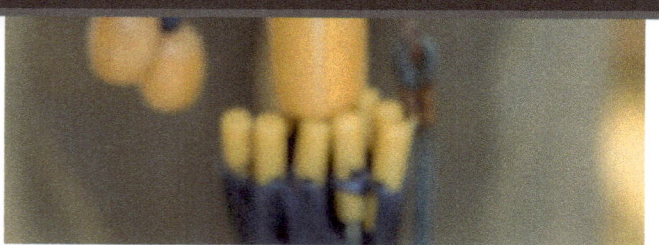

A family heirloom...tragically mislaid. Can it be found?

This is a very personal rewiring, penned by Mike.

. . . .

My wife, Valerie, is extraordinarily beautiful. And kind. And forgiving—which is helpful being married to me.

She's also organized. (Helpful again!)

She's loving and considerate, saintly even.

I need to get all that out of the way, because while it's true, it's maybe not the whole story.

She does have a short suit.

She is not the tidiest person in God's creation.

Full of the Spirit, yes. Full of the tidy-bug, no.

The absence of the gift of tidiness, with which I am not altogether blessed either, it must be said, has led to a tendency for her to mislay things. (There we are perfectly complemented, as I have the gift for finding, so that's all good.)

With one notable and tragic exception.

Nearly 20 years after our wedding day, she mislaid her wedding ring in our home in Kent in Southeast England.

It was not any old ring. I had not bought it from a jewelry shop. (Her engagement ring had come from a bar-

gain basement jeweler's at a cost of just £13—all the money I had aged 19 and yet to start a job. But that is by the by.)

The wedding ring was special. It had been handed down to her by her grandmother and so was irreplaceable.

As I say, I have been blessed with the gift of finding, so I knew all would be well.

But, more than 20 years later, I'm still searching.

Gold is virtually indestructible. And it doesn't tarnish or deteriorate. So, the galling thing is that Valerie and I both know it exists somewhere, shiny, waiting to be discovered.

It may be that thousands of years from now it will be retrieved from the ditch or jackdaw nest in which it has laid secreted for millennia, and a futuristic version of television's Time Team archaeologists will excavate and value it.

Meantime, Valerie has a new ring, blessed and dedicated at our silver wedding anniversary.

But equally we both still live in hope that, one day, we may find the original.

If we do, I can promise you that we shall have the party to end all parties!

The parable of the lost coin

Luke
15:8-10

⁸"Or suppose a woman has ten silver coins and loses one. Doesn't she light a lamp, sweep the house and search carefully until she finds it? ⁹And when she finds it, she calls her friends and neighbors together and says, 'Rejoice with me; I have found my lost coin.' ¹⁰In the same way, I tell you, there is rejoicing in the presence of the angels of God over one sinner who repents."

So, what's this story saying to US, here and now?

What we really like about the "lost parables" is that the protagonists do not sit still, passively bemoaning the loss. They desperately search for it.

Here, the woman turns her house upside down to find her lost coin.

(The coin may have formed part of her wedding head-dress, which like Valerie's lost ring, would have made it extra precious.)

Previously, we've seen the shepherd heading for the hills to hunt for his lost sheep.

Plot spoiler alert: in the next parable, the father looks out every day for his errant son, and when he sees him in the distance, rushes out to meet him and bring him home.

Meanwhile, 20 years on, Valerie and Mike are still hunting for her ring.

How wonderful to think that God is desperately looking for each and every one of his prodigal children.

If, in this strange world of spiritual hide-and-seek that so many of us choose to play, you've not let him find you yet, maybe it's time to come out from behind the couch. Be assured. God's not going to give up looking.

In fact, he'll do whatever it takes.

2,000 years ago, he even took on human form.

And maybe he's asking you to help him find a particular someone today.

Reflection and prayer | How hard am I searching?

. . . .

_____

_____

_____

_____

_____

_____

What's this story saying to **me,** here and now?

. . . .

_____

_____

_____

_____

_____

_____

THE TALE OF THE
TEENAGE WASTREL

Split out on his fam...to taste the (not so) good life. Will he find his way home?

This third parable in the "Lost" sequence is about a son, lost to his father and lost to himself:

. . . .

If you ever find yourself in the backstreets of Oldham in the north of England, try to find your way to Clarendon Street and look at the garage you'll find there: Butterworth and Co. Apart from being an honest, well-run, family business, it has an interesting story to tell.

The father and owner, John, worked hard throughout the eighties and nineties to build his business, which acquired a strong reputation for restoring and maintaining classic cars: Ferraris, Porsches and, their speciality, American Mustangs and Cobras. Granted, there weren't too many of these sorts of cars cruising around the streets of Oldham, but they required specialist mechanics, and there weren't too many of those around either! His two children, Sharon and Lee, learned these specialist skills alongside their father, and the plan was to expand the business, with Sharon and Lee each opening their own outlets, funded by their father.

John found their first suitable site in Leeds, and Sharon set to work. It was hard going but she stuck at it. Signs were that in a few years it would be a very profitable business. Meanwhile, John had identified another site, this one in Liverpool, and earmarked it for Lee when his apprenticeship was finished.

But Lee had other ideas. Fired up by the Mustangs and Cobras, his mind was set on Los Angeles, a cool city with lots of classic cars on the streets. On his 18th birthday, and without saying anything to his father or Sharon, he transferred $250,000 from the company's business bank account into his personal account. "I'm of age now, and it will be mine anyway when the old man dies," he reasoned, "so it's only like he's died a bit before his time."

So, Lee set off for the big city, and he loved it. He found an apartment in Beverly Hills, much more expensive than he had anticipated, but what the heck. Looking at the number of classic cars adorning the streets, the money would soon be rolling in. And what a place to live! Girls, restaurants, a classic car of his own, and Las Vegas was just a four-hour drive across the desert. He'd never experienced the delights of blackjack, fine champagne, and a blonde on his arm in Oldham! He hired some experienced mechanics to do the grubby work while he concentrated on flying the high life.

But a time bomb was ticking. Whereas he had been well apprenticed in the art of servicing classic cars, no one had taken Lee through the intricacies of the cash flows, profit and loss summaries, and the balance sheets involved in running a business. Moreover, while he had slavered over the sight of so many classic cars on the street, he had not realized that the consequence would be a plethora of garages specializing in restoring and maintaining them.

While he was running up a personal debt mountain in Vegas, a consequence of a cocktail of hotel bills, gambling losses, and the expenses of a growing drink and drugs addiction; his business ran into the red, ran out of cash, and ran up losses that its assets would not cover. In short, he was bankrupt. Worse than that, he was in hock to Caesar's Palace to the tune of thousands of dollars. He thought of contacting his father, but shame and fear of what he would say prevented him. He would just have to take what was coming to him.

In Los Angeles, his business was liquidated by the authorities. In Vegas, his passport was confiscated, and he agreed to do a five-year custodial stint in the kitchens of Caesar's Palace to pay off a small proportion of his debts there. Every day he cursed the boyish naivety that had led him into this mess, and every day he wondered how his father and elder sister were getting on back home. At this point, even Oldham sounded attractive.

He wrote home regularly. He gave no hint of his actual state of affairs, especially his current incarceration, but he resolved to return home once he had completed his five years. After all, he reasoned, the only job he knew was restoring classic cars, and as his future now lay in working for someone else, he may as well do that to help his father's business.

Come the day, he bought a discounted one-way ticket to Manchester, wrote to his father to let him know he would be coming back, and explained all the circumstances.

Arriving at Ringway Airport, he was surprised and amazed to see his father waiting for him at the Arrivals barrier, carrying a big 'welcome home' sign, which he dropped as soon as he saw his son. His dad vaulted over the barriers and ran down the Arrivals Hall, dodging other arriving passengers as he did so.

In a scene that could have been cut directly from *Love Actually*, father and son fell into each other's arms. "Dad, I feel so stupid and so ashamed. I've wasted all the money you worked so hard to make. I know it's all my fault, and I wouldn't blame you if you just told me to get lost, but can I just come back and work for you?

I probably won't ever be able to pay it all back, but at least I can try."

To Lee's utter amazement, all his father did was hug him tighter and cry a little. Wiping away the tears, he replied, "Yes, of course you can come back. Forget about the money. It's not important. We'll create another pot of capital for you, and before too long, you'll be up and running in Liverpool or wherever else you like, except for Los Angeles! Meanwhile, I have that bottle of vintage champagne your grandfather left me on ice at home, so let's get back and celebrate!"

Back home, Lee found a big welcome party waiting to greet him. He disappeared upstairs to drop his things into his old room. Meanwhile, Sharon accosted her father. "Dad, what on earth are you doing? Lee robs you of your cash, deserts us to run off to the States, and has a fine old time, while I've been working round the clock to help you build the business. Not once have we stopped to celebrate like this. What's gotten into you?"

"Sharon," his father replied, "I know what you're saying and why. I really do love and appreciate you. This business is as much yours as mine. But I thought I'd lost my son, your brother, and I'm just so glad he's back. I can't think of much else I'd rather celebrate more."

The parable of the prodigal son

Luke
15:11-32

[11]Jesus continued: "There was a man who had two sons. [12]The younger one said to his father, 'Father, give me my share of the estate.' So, he divided his property between them.

[13]"Not long after that, the younger son got together all he had, set off for a distant country and there squandered his wealth in wild living. [14]After he had spent everything, there was a severe famine in that whole country, and he began to be in need. [15]So he went and hired himself out to a citizen of that country, who sent him to his fields to feed pigs. [16]He longed to fill his stomach with the pods that the pigs were eating, but no one gave him anything.

[17]"When he came to his senses, he said, 'How many of my father's hired servants have food to spare, and here I am starving to death! [18]I will set out and go back to my father and say to him: Father, I have sinned against heaven and against you. [19]I am no longer worthy to be called your son; make me like one of your hired servants.' [20]So he got up and went to his father.

"But while he was still a long way off, his father saw him and was filled with compassion for him; he ran to his son, threw his arms around him and kissed him.

[21]"The son said to him, 'Father, I have sinned against heaven and against you. I am no longer worthy to be called your son.'

[22]"But the father said to his servants, 'Quick! Bring the best robe and put it on him. Put a ring on his finger and sandals on his feet. [23]Bring the fattened calf and kill it. Let's have a feast and celebrate. [24]For this son of mine was dead and is alive again; he was lost and is found.' So, they began to celebrate.

[25]"Meanwhile, the older son was in the field. When he came near the house, he heard music and dancing. [26]So he called one of the servants and asked him what was going on. [27]'Your brother has come,' he replied, 'and your father has killed the fattened calf because he has him back safe and sound.'

[28]"The older brother became angry and refused to go in. So, his father went out and pleaded with him. [29]But he answered his father, 'Look! All these years I've been slaving for you and never disobeyed your orders. Yet you never gave me even a young goat so I could celebrate with my friends. [30]But when this son of yours who has squandered your property with prostitutes comes home, you kill the fattened calf for him!'

[31]"'My son,' the father said, 'you are always with me, and everything I have is yours. [32]But we had to celebrate and be glad, because this brother of yours was dead and is alive again; he was lost and is found.'"

So, what's this story saying to US, here and now?

This is one of Jesus' best-known parables.

Some people find it helpful to look at it from the absconding son's perspective, others from the father's, and still others from the elder son's (or, in the case of our rewiring, the elder sister's) perspective. Some people like to take their time and consider it from all three points of view.

See which works best for you.

For us, there is one strong and central message that stands out.

However far you may feel that you have drifted away from God, there is always a way back. Not only that, but God is constantly looking out for you and will even come to meet you where you are.

Like many people, Mike first encountered God as a child. He had a Bible and went to Sunday school. But, when he started to become more independent as an older teenager, he began to drift away. God no longer seemed so relevant to his life. When he packed his bags and left home to start work, he also packed his spiritual bags and put them in storage.

But, twenty years later, a set of circumstances caused him to dig out those bags and head back to God. And there God was, waiting for him, as if he'd never been away. Actually, he wasn't just waiting, he was running towards Mike with as many tears in his eyes as Mike had in his.

All Mike had to do was say "I'm sorry," and God took it from there.

Ivan's story is similar yet different. He went to Sunday school as a kid, but like Mike, he drifted away from God. By the time Ivan was 17, God didn't figure in his life at all. Compared to music, money, and girls, God neither seemed real nor relevant.

In Ivan's case, God chased him down.

One day, Ivan was strumming his guitar in his home, working on some song lyrics, when God gave him a compelling vision in his mind. It was unlike any thought Ivan had ever had before. It was gripping. Ivan had not thought about church for ages. Yet, in the vision, he saw himself, now as a 17-year-old kid, sitting in exactly the same pew as he had as a five-year-old at Sunday school.

As Ivan pondered this captivating mental image, two powerful thoughts came to his mind. The first was that he needed to investigate Jesus as an adult to figure out what was true. The second shocked him even more. All of a sudden, Ivan had an overwhelming desire to be pure, not a concept he had given much thought to as a teenage boy; yet, in that nanosecond, he knew he had offended God and had to sort out his life.

Ivan never thought of going to church. Instead, he went to the local library, borrowed books about Jesus, read them, fell in love with Jesus, and has been a Jesus follower ever since. While "sorry" might sometimes be the hardest word, it's one of the most life changing ones.

Try it!

There must be millions of people in America that have not rejected God, but have simply drifted away from him, millions of people just like us two, although probably better looking.

If you are one of them, then this parable is for you.

Millions of others must feel they have offended God or are just not good enough to be accepted by him.

If you are one of them, this parable is for you too.

God wants you back home.

All it takes is a meaningful "sorry" (or as the Bible puts it elsewhere, "a broken heart and a contrite spirit").

Reflection and prayer | Am I 'far from home'?

What's this story saying to **me,** here and now?

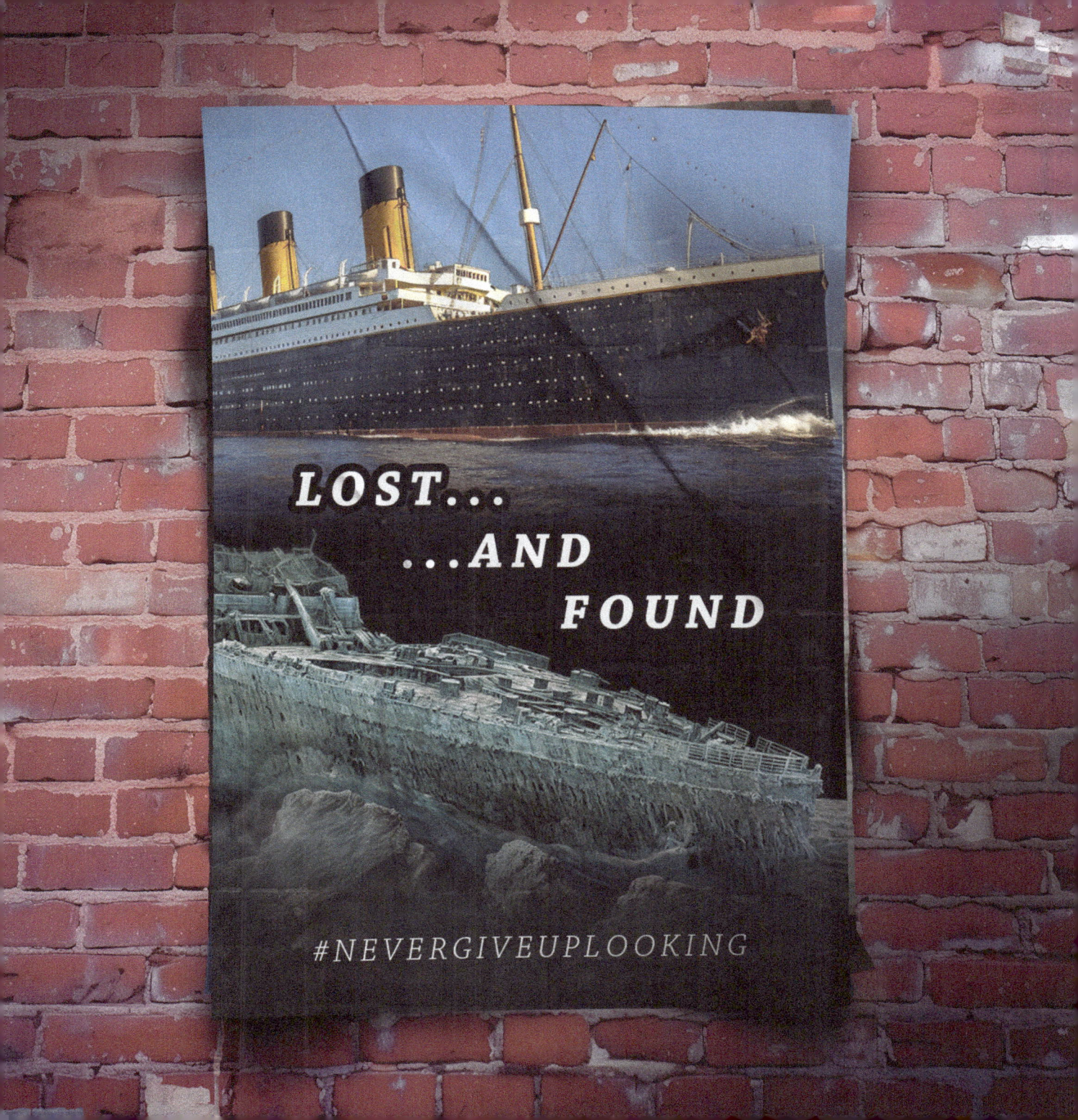

To be completely and utterly lost can be profoundly disturbing.

Equally, to lose something precious can be profoundly distressing.

These parables enable us to experience the sense of loss from both perspectives.

Mike remembers once losing touch with his young daughter, Georgina, in a crowd.

She freaked out and he freaked out.

When reunited both were in tears.

Ivan has an appalling sense of direction.

He's been lost in Mexico City, several European cities, and even the Père Lachaise Cemetery in Paris.

Ivan is used to being lost, but also used to being found.

Being found is better.

When we lose touch with God, it disturbs us.

When we lose touch with God, it distresses God.

The good thing is that God never loses touch with us.

So, there is always a way back.

And God is always there, waiting.

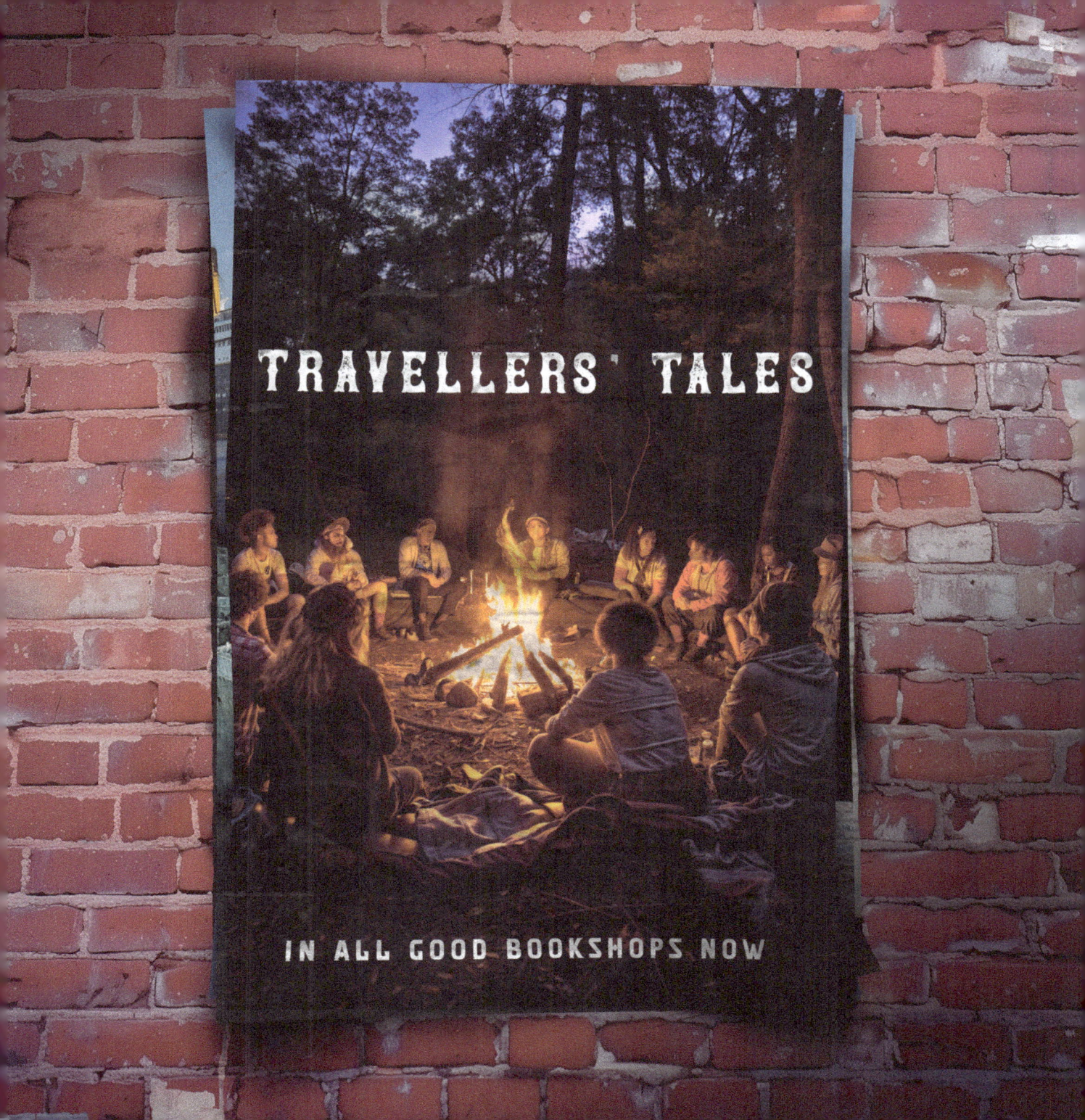

Canterbury is the birthplace of Christianity in England. It's where St. Augustine arrived in 597 at the behest of Pope Gregory the Great. His mission: to bring the Gospel to that heathen land.

In 1170, Canterbury Cathedral was the scene of the murder of Archbishop Thomas Becket: a man who dared to come between church and state.

(You can read all about it in TS Eliot's classic play: 'Murder in the Cathedral')

After his death, Becket's tomb and relics drew pilgrims from all over Europe, and in 1173 he was canonised by the Pope. In the centuries since, countless people have made a pilgrimage to Canterbury from all over the world.

(They still do. Mike worships at the Cathedral and sees such groups arrive every week.)

Those ancient pilgrims travelled in groups over many days, weeks, months.

Along the way they told stories to pass the time.

Geoffery Chaucer related such stories in his epic 14th century block-buster novel: *Canterbury Tales.*

These tales are moralistic, earthy, and rooted in, but often challenging, the prevailing culture.

The sort of stories Jesus liked to tell.

The sort of stories he told on his last journey up to Jerusalem:

> A story that had a touch of the supernatural about it. The Rich Man and Lazarus.

> A story that turned social order on its head. The Workers in the Vineyard.

> A story that dared to puncture religious pomposity and hypocrisy. The Pharisee and the Tax Collector.

> And a story which challenges each of us to use or lose the skills with which we have been blessed. The Talents.

The sort of stories that would have salted and sweetened the journey time to Jerusalem then, and will salt and sweeten each of us on our continuing faith journeys.

So, wherever you are in your faith journey: dismissive, resistant, curious, hesitant; taking tiny first steps, making big strides and giant leaps; or anywhere outside, betwixt or between; these stories will have something to say to you and help you travel well.

THE STORY OF THE SASSY THEME PARK MANAGER

A not-so-fun park...where the only things riding the big dipper...are the profits. Can the kingdom rediscover its magic?

"The King of Fun."

That's what they call Albert Tomkins.

Born in the first half of the 20th century, he has managed to stretch himself out towards his centenary in the 21st.

He claims he has now forgotten more than he ever learned, but the lie of that can be found in the way that, even in his 92nd year, he keeps a tight grip upon his business empire.

Maybe that is because his empire is all about fun, amusement parks to be exact, of which he has six, dotted around the country.

But not all his parks at the moment are fun. In fact, one is being a real pain.

The park in the Twin Cities is seeing admissions down, revenues down, and profits wiped out.

Sure, there are mitigating circumstances: weather (it's either too hot or too cold), road construction (three seasons of the year), competition, and the economy. But Albert never has been nor ever will be the mitigating type.

So, Miranda Sherburn, the commercial manager of the park, knew she was skating on thinner and thinner ice.

Albert had made this clear: "Write your profit up or your resignation down. You have four weeks."

Miranda was in despair. The operational product, rides, catering, and so forth, was controlled centrally. She had no input to those. So, too, were the admission prices. She could not affect those.

Or could she?

She was desperate. She could feel the axe blade cold against her neck. "OK," she thought, "I can't change prices, but I could change our rebate policy. I'm not sure I'm allowed to do that. In fact, I'm really sure I'm not, but what the heck? I need to get people in here. There's no way I'll get a job elsewhere with this place looking like a locked-down city after a curfew."

So, everyone who came in was given an immediate 50% reduction on their admission fee because some parts of the park "were still under construction." Children under 11 were admitted free of charge.

Miranda thought, it's Albert's park, so it's his money. He's not going to miss a few bucks. The main thing is, if admissions pick up, it will play well on my resume when Albert fires me for what I've done.

Sure enough, visitors told family and friends about this fantastic value for money. A local celebrity with a large following on social media tweeted about it and liked the park's Facebook page.

Word got around, admissions increased, and Miranda didn't know whether to be pleased or terrified.

One day, Albert paid a surprise visit. To inspect the books.

To Miranda's complete surprise, he was delighted. "Footfall!" he exclaimed. "Admissions. Users. Whatever you want to call them. They are all on the up! Well done!

"The key to any business is to get people aware of, and interested in, your product. To persuade them to try it. Then it's down to product quality. Make that good enough, and they'll come back again. And profit will follow.

"You've created interest in this fun park. Now all we need to do is convert them into loyal, repeat customers.

"You can leave that to me. Your job is to keep on attracting them."

The parable of the shrewd steward

Luke
16:1-8

[1]*Jesus told his disciples: "There was a rich man whose manager was accused of wasting his possessions.* [2]*So he called him in and asked him, 'What is this I hear about you? Give an account of your management, because you cannot be manager any longer.'*

[3]*"The manager said to himself, 'What shall I do now? My master is taking away my job. I'm not strong enough to dig, and I'm ashamed to beg—* [4]*I know what I'll do so that, when I lose my job here, people will welcome me into their houses.'*

[5]*"So he called in each one of his master's debtors. He asked the first, 'How much do you owe my master?'*

[6]*"'Nine hundred gallons of olive oil,' he replied.*

"The manager told him, 'Take your bill, sit down quickly, and make it four hundred and fifty.'

[7]*"Then he asked the second, 'And how much do you owe?'*

"'A thousand bushels of wheat,' he replied.

"He told him, 'Take your bill and make it eight hundred.'

[8]*"The master commended the dishonest manager because he had acted shrewdly. For the people of this world are more shrewd in dealing with their own kind than are the people of the light.*

So, what's this story saying to US, here and now?

What a strange parable. What an odd message.

On the surface.

The principal character is called a shrewd manager. Some of us might be tempted to call him something else!

So, what point is Jesus trying to make?

Well, in our rewiring we've tried to bring out the importance of adapting central policy in the light of on-the-ground, tactical expertise.

The big multinational marketing companies have a phrase for it: "Think global; act local."

The church is a wonderful institution, full of devoted ministers.

But like many institutions, it can occasionally lose touch with life outside it and live in its own "bubble."

Devoted church ministers are not necessarily exposed to real-world conditions in the same way as their parishioners. No criticism intended—just a challenge.

Maybe we parishioners are better placed to speak into the workplaces and social circles that we inhabit and know first-hand.

Maybe God is calling us to say and do whatever it takes to bring people to him.

To be shrewd managers and fill his amusement park.

Reflection and prayer | Am I bursting the bubble?

· ·

_____

_____

_____

_____

_____

_____

What's this story saying to **me,** here and now?

· ·

_____

_____

_____

_____

_____

_____

A TALE OF TWO LANDLORDS

780

782

CRATCHIT & PARTNERS
FOR RENT
WWW.CRATCHITANDPARTNERS.COM
Contract Pending

SCROOGE & SONS
REALTY
FOR RENT
WWW.SCROOGEANDSONS.COM
UNIT AVAILABLE

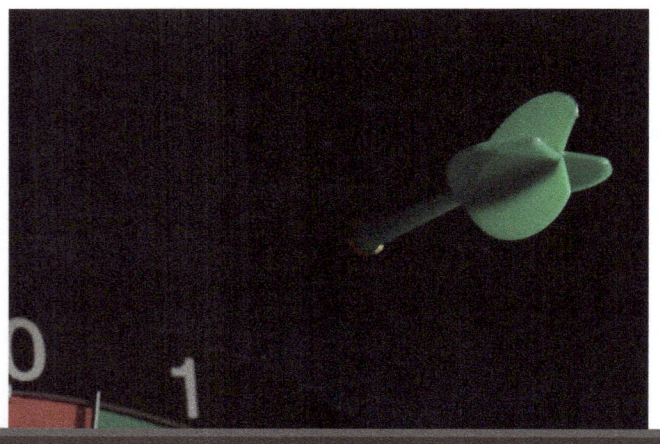

When Cratchit...has the last laugh on Scrooge. What the Dickens is going on?

Many of Jesus' stories were rooted in ordinary, everyday life. Others were allegorical. This is one of them. Jesus knew just how to hit a raw nerve, forcing his listeners to think about how their everyday life choices have eternal consequences. It's a real zinger.

In the closing years of the last century many people in the UK started to build up property portfolios. Soaring property prices meant it was a win-win game: capital appreciation and rental income.

This is a tale of two men who jumped on the bandwagon.

But with very different business philosophies.

Scrooge's objective was to make as much money as possible. Full stop. The houses and his tenants were simply a means to that end and were treated accordingly. Houses were renovated as cheaply as possible and maintained in the same way, if at all. Tenancy agreements were written entirely in Scrooge's favor, allowing him to terminate and evict at will. Deposits were, of course, never returned.

Cratchit saw his purpose as providing a service to his tenants. Tenancy agreements were fair and exceeded all the legal requirements for protecting tenants' rights. Houses were renovated and maintained to the highest standards. Cratchit's philosophy was to provide accommodations that he himself would be happy to live in.

Both men focused their businesses on Canterbury in Southeast England, a heritage city with a Cathedral and a large and transient student and young professional population. So, they were constantly competing for properties and tenants. Scrooge's lower renovation and non-existent maintenance costs meant that he could take great delight in gazumping Cratchit on house purchases and undercutting him on rentals. His objective was to squeeze Cratchit out of the business so that he could buy up his assets at a knock-down price.

This fierce competition led both men to re-invest all their profits in their businesses.

And why not? What could possibly go wrong?

In 2007 they found out the answer to that question.

The bank-led financial crisis caused a crash in property prices and a freeze on mortgage lending.

Almost overnight, win-win became lose-lose. Many property speculators saw their businesses destroyed as banks foreclosed and crystallized negative equity. Scrooge and Cratchit were among their number. Their world moved from the benefits of business to the business of benefits, unemployment benefits!

But just a couple of months later, Scrooge saw that Cratchit was back in the property market. He raged and cursed. How could this be?

His investigations revealed that Cratchit had received a large grant from the Property Landlords Association. Immediately Scrooge applied for a similar grant, and immediately he was refused. Immediately he demanded a meeting with them.

He stormed into their offices, and his temper worsened as, while sitting in reception, he could see Cratchit through the glass walls enjoying tea and cake and talking with the Chairman in what was obviously a very affable meeting.

Scrooge was then shown into the office of the Grants Director. No tea was offered and certainly no cake. The essence of the case Scrooge made was that his business was much bigger than Cratchit's, and so he should get a correspondingly larger grant.

The Grants Director was not impressed.

"The size of a business has no bearing on whether or not we make a grant. That decision is based solely on how a landlord scores in the tenant satisfaction surveys that we carry out.

"It may interest you to know that Mr. Cratchit has topped that survey for the past five years and that is why we immediately gave him a grant. Half a million pounds at no interest and payable back over 20 years." Scrooge's eyes bulged. "Mr. Cratchit is good for the reputation of our industry, and we want him back in business. It may also interest you to know, Mr. Scrooge, that you have been consistently bottom of our survey by some distance. In fact, you were hardly on the scale. You, Mr. Scrooge, are the type of person we do not want in our industry. You bring us all into disrepute."

This stinging rebuke was made even more unpalatable for Scrooge by his being able to see Cratchit across the corridor taking another piece of cake and enjoying a joke with the Chairman.

He changed tack. "Well, if not me, could you make a grant to my close associates, the Marleys? My son works with them. I now understand how you see things and will join them to ensure they change their working practices. Please also send Cratchit to talk to them and explain how you want them to operate."

"No, Mr. Scrooge. We have talked regularly with the Marleys over the years, asking them to change their business practices. As they chose not to listen then, I see no reason why they would listen now, even if we were to send Mr. Cratchit as living, breathing evidence of the value in doing so.

"I'm sorry, Sir, there is to be no grant from this Association for you, the Marleys, or any others of your ilk."

The parable of the rich man and Lazarus

Luke
16:19-31

¹⁹"There was a rich man who was dressed in purple and fine linen and lived in luxury every day. ²⁰At his gate was laid a beggar named Lazarus, covered with sores ²¹and longing to eat what fell from the rich man's table. Even the dogs came and licked his sores.

²²"The time came when the beggar died and the angels carried him to Abraham's side. The rich man also died and was buried. ²³In Hades, where he was in torment, he looked up and saw Abraham far away, with Lazarus by his side. ²⁴So he called to him, 'Father Abraham, have pity on me and send Lazarus to dip the tip of his finger in water and cool my tongue, because I am in agony in this fire.'

²⁵"But Abraham replied, 'Son, remember that in your lifetime you received your good things, while Lazarus received bad things, but now he is comforted here and you are in agony. ²⁶And besides all this, between us and you a great chasm has been set in place, so that those who want to go from here to you cannot, nor can anyone cross over from there to us.'

²⁷"He answered, 'Then I beg you, father, send Lazarus to my family, ²⁸for I have five brothers. Let him warn them, so that they will not also come to this place of torment.'

²⁹"Abraham replied, 'They have Moses and the Prophets; let them listen to them.'

³⁰"'No, father Abraham,' he said, 'but if someone from the dead goes to them, they will repent.'

³¹"He said to him, 'If they do not listen to Moses and the Prophets, they will not be convinced even if someone rises from the dead.'"

So, what's this story saying to US, here and now?

This parable has a touch of the "Tales of the Supernatural" about it.

It is also one of the harshest stories that Jesus told.

Normally he would tell people there was still time to heed his message.

Even for the criminal who was dying on the cross next to him.

But here, he is very clear that time runs out when you die and that, once dead, you can't turn the clock back.

Millions of Americans have not rejected Jesus; they have just not got around to accepting him yet.

But the message here is stark and clear.

If you are someone who is putting your faith decision off until tomorrow, just bear in mind that one day tomorrow won't come.

Reflection and prayer | Is time slipping through my hands?

· ·

_____

_____

_____

_____

_____

What's this story saying to me, **here and now?**

· ·

_____

_____

_____

_____

_____

THE LABORERS ON
THE BUILDING SITE

When the first to show...are the last to get paid. Are they happy with that?

Jesus has just been quite tough on a young man who has his priorities in life all out of sync. He can sense his disciples are having a crisis of confidence about whether even they are good enough for Heaven. So, he tells them this story:

. . . .

Tomasz Glik, the owner of a building construction firm in Portland, Maine, was delighted to win the contract for a new sports and leisure center. The first task was to prepare the site. This was not as easy as it might sound since a pig farm previously occupied it, and dozens of concrete sties still littered the area in varying states of disrepair. Moreover, access was restricted, making it impossible to get the normal earth-moving equipment onto the site. This was a job for good old-fashioned grunt work! And so, Tomasz put the word about that he was on the lookout for a few heavies. He was keen to get the site cleared, and he reckoned a day's work on the site should do it.

Early the next morning he found a dozen men outside the site. They agreed a rate of $200 for the day's work, and they got themselves stuck in. By the time the first coffee break came around it was clear that these guys were good workers. It was equally clear, however, that there weren't enough of them to finish the job that day. So, Tomasz took a stroll into town and found the local employment agency. There was another dozen men there that fitted the bill, so he signed them on, agreeing that, although they would not be doing a full day's work, he would nevertheless pay them a fair rate.

Partway through the day, a sudden downpour hit, turning the site to mud and making it obvious that yet more workers would be required. Tomasz went back into town and found half a dozen Latinos playing checkers in a cafe. Two further trips to a couple of bars generated another ten, a mix of Bulgarians, Romanians, and Latvians. But late in the day, he knew he needed a final boost for the last couple of hours. He found his labor in the shape of five strapping young local lads returning from a day's fishing. That did the trick. By the time the light was failing at 9.00 pm the site was clear.

Tomasz called his site foreman over and asked him to pay the laborers starting with the last ones "recruited" and finishing with the first.

The foreman gave $200 to each of the young lads who had been grabbed as they returned from their fishing trip. At this, the early morning starters became very excited as they anticipated a bumper pay-out. But, in fact, every laborer received the same $200 wage. The early starters sought out Tomasz to register their dissatisfaction. "What's the deal? The guys you brought on site at the end of the day only worked a couple of hours, but you've treated them the same as us, and we worked through the whole day, rain and all. That isn't fair!"

"Hold on," said Tomasz. "I'm not being unfair to you. I agreed to pay you $200, and that's what I've done. You were okay with that then, and you should be okay with it now. If I want to be generous and give the lads who came last the same amount, surely that's my concern. It's my money, and I'm just pleased we all got the job done together."

The parable of the workers in the vineyard

Matthew 20:1-16

¹"For the kingdom of heaven is like a landowner who went out early in the morning to hire workers for his vineyard. ²He agreed to pay them a denarius for the day and sent them into his vineyard.

³"About nine in the morning he went out and saw others standing in the marketplace doing nothing. ⁴He told them, 'You also go and work in my vineyard, and I will pay you whatever is right.' ⁵So they went.

"He went out again about noon and about three in the afternoon and did the same thing. ⁶About five in the afternoon he went out and found still others standing around. He asked them, 'Why have you been standing here all day long doing nothing?'

⁷"'Because no one has hired us,' they answered.

"He said to them, 'You also go and work in my vineyard.'

⁸"When evening came, the owner of the vineyard said to his foreman, 'Call the workers and pay them their wages, beginning with the last ones hired and going on to the first.'

⁹"The workers who were hired about five in the afternoon came and each received a denarius. ¹⁰So when those came who were hired first, they expected to receive more. But each one of them also received a denarius. ¹¹When they received it, they began to grumble against the landowner. ¹²'These who were hired last worked only one hour,' they said, 'and you have made them equal to us who have borne the burden of the work and the heat of the day.'

¹³"But he answered one of them, 'I am not being unfair to you, friend. Didn't you agree to work for a denarius? ¹⁴Take your pay and go. I want to give the one who was hired last the same as I gave you. ¹⁵Don't I have the right to do what I want with my own money? Or are you envious because I am generous?'

¹⁶"So the last will be first, and the first will be last."

So, what's this story saying to US, here and now?

This story tells us lots of things.

First thought. In God's eyes, people are valued in the absolute terms of their own worth rather than relative to others.

The last can indeed be first and the first last, except that with God, there is no first and last!

Those of us who are Christians should try to value people likewise. It is not for us to judge or condemn, to say who is or isn't worthy of Heaven. It is for us to encourage and welcome.

If ever we measure ourselves against others, we invariably invite trouble: berating ourselves for not being as good as them or condemning them for not being as good as us.

God values everyone equally, so maybe we should do the same.

Second thought. Heaven has no maximum capacity, and latecomers are every bit as welcome as early birds.

In the story, the latecomers to the vineyard and building site could easily have said "no" because they were too tired, had better things to do, wanted to eat, or simply because they'd had a bad day and it sounded too much like hard work. They may have thought they would not earn enough money to make it worthwhile anyway. But they chose to say "yes" and gained a reward as good as the early arrivals.

No one is ever too late or too old to become a Christian, as the thief crucified alongside Jesus discovered.

Third thought. Heaven is not an exclusive establishment.

We cannot earn or buy our way in. Entry is completely at God's discretion, by his grace.

Unlike the local golf club, yacht club, or masonic lodge, there is no selection committee, no people we need to impress, no waiting lists, no priority applications.

Heaven is open to all who put their faith and trust in Jesus.

Fourth thought. There is no long line to join, waiting for the doors to open. Truth be told, God searches us out, knocks on the door of our hearts, and invites us in.

He is still knocking.

Listen up!

Reflection and prayer | Is Heaven knock, knock, knocking at my door?

- -

_____

_____

_____

_____

_____

_____

What's this story saying to me, here and now?

- -

_____

_____

_____

_____

_____

_____

_____

THE REFEREE'S TALE

The on-field decision...is challenged off-field. Who referees the referee?

Jesus spent three years with his twelve disciples, a really extended coaching session! He knew that the future of the church depended on these guys. Here's something he taught them about prayer:

· ·

Michelle Blackwell shivered, checked her watch, tested her whistle, and looked around.

A hundred spectators? Maybe 150?

A far cry from the 75,000 or more just two weeks ago.

But that had been in Paris, France, where she had refereed the Women's Soccer World Cup semi-final: Germany taking on England.

Kalamazoo at Grand Rapids in the Michigan Women's U 15 Soccer League was never going to attract the world's media, particularly on a mud bath of a pitch under unremittingly grey and freezing skies.

But this was where she had refereed her first game 20 years ago to the day, and so she had accepted an invitation to return and referee the state derby match to mark the occasion.

It was good to return to her roots, and she was looking forward to catching up with some old school friends in the clubhouse afterwards.

An hour and a half later, a mediocre game with no goals was nearing the final minutes, and Michelle was anticipating her hot shower, when one of the Kalama-

zoo players intercepted a back pass and sprinted towards the Grand Rapids goal. With only the goalkeeper to beat, she body-swerved but then crashed to the ground.

Michelle's whistle shrieked long and hard. She sprinted across to the Grand Rapids keeper, scowling, pointing to the penalty spot, and flourishing her red card. A trip was unacceptable at any level of the game. Not in Paris. Not at Wembley in England. And not in Grand Rapids. The keeper protested that she had not touched the player, that her opponent had beaten her but had then slipped in the mud.

Michelle would have none of it, and the goalkeeper trudged off the pitch, muttering and gesticulating.

The player's teammates claimed furiously that there had been no physical contact. Michelle would have none of that either. She was used to team pressure.

A group of spectators, mainly Grand Rapids parents, joined the protest. Vociferously.

Again, Michelle would have none of it. They were clearly biased to the home player.

The Kalamazoo captain took the penalty against a stand-in keeper. She skied it way over the bar leaving the final score at 0-0, a fitting end to a drab game. Michelle blew the final whistle and headed for the clubhouse.

On the way, the "tripped" Kalamazoo player took Michelle to one side and explained that she felt she had simply slipped.

Still, Michelle would have none of it. She knew what she had seen. It was a trip, and she was an experienced international soccer referee, one of the top refs in the world.

There was no way she could get such a decision wrong. Except that, in this case, she had.

She found the Grand Rapids keeper waiting for her outside the clubhouse to protest her innocence again.

Michelle's response was to inform her she would be reporting her to the National Women's U 15 Soccer League, and that she could expect a two-game ban.

When Michelle emerged from her dressing room, she found the distraught goalie still there with several of her teammates in support.

Michelle resolutely turned her back on them and headed for the clubhouse.

She was halfway through her first hot chocolate when the Grand Rapids deputation reappeared, swelled by more spectators, parents, and players all claiming that Michelle had made a grave error.

Michelle started to lose her temper, and when a group of Kalamazoo players and parents joined the dissent against her decision, she exploded and stormed out towards her car.

But once outside she reflected. Top international official she might be, but the level of protest was passionate, widespread, and seemingly sincere. Not one voice had been raised in support of her decision. Maybe, just maybe, she had got this one wrong.

Time for some grace and humility.

Michelle returned to the clubhouse. "Normally, I would use the video system to review my decision, but clearly, we don't have that luxury here. However, I guess human eyes can be as good as any technology, and I have been swayed by your consistency and unanimity, but mostly by your sheer persistence. I therefore reverse my decision. The cookies and shakes are on me."

The parable of the persistent widow

Luke
18:1-7

¹Then Jesus told his disciples a parable to show them that they should always pray and not give up. ²He said: "In a certain town there was a judge who neither feared God nor cared what people thought. ³And there was a widow in that town who kept coming to him with the plea,

'Grant me justice against my adversary.'

⁴"For some time he refused. But finally he said to himself, 'Even though I don't fear God or care what people think, ⁵yet because this widow keeps bothering me,

I will see that she gets justice, so that she won't eventually come and attack me!'"

⁶And the Lord said, "Listen to what the unjust judge says. ⁷And will not God bring about justice for his chosen ones, who cry out to him day and night? Will he keep putting them off?"

So, what's this story saying to US, here and now?

It's always great to talk about answered prayer, isn't it? So, we tend to make a point of sharing our answered prayers with others.

But we are never quite so keen to talk about our unanswered prayers.

Some people will say that there is no such thing as unanswered prayer.

But in this parable, Jesus is urging his disciples to be persistent in their prayers, even if they seem unanswered. Jesus urges them to pray, pray, and pray again.

But if they need to keep on praying, surely it means that the prayer has not yet been answered.

Why might that be? Why might a prayer go unanswered?

We can suggest several reasons. Maybe it's because the answer doesn't come in the timeframe we expect. So, when we get to see the answer, we no longer connect it to a particular prayer.

Perhaps the answer doesn't come in the manner we expect. So, again, we don't connect the answer to the prayer request.

Sometimes our prayers are so vague that we'd have no idea if God answered them or not.

Possibly God wants us to continue praying because that is helpful for us. Prayer is a conversation with God, so prolonged prayer may not be such a bad thing! People of strong faith are invariably people of strong prayer and vice versa.

Maybe it's because of a lack of real faith on our part.

Are we praying more in hope than expectation? If this is the case, the only thing we can do is ask Jesus to give us faith. We can't magic it up, but like the persistent widow, we can keep asking for it. And faith is a little like the Red Carpet. Jesus loves to walk down it when he sees faith.

Or perhaps something is getting in the way.

Parents will know the problems of dealing with a disobedient or rebellious child. "Sorry" before "please" is often the response to a plea for a new toy or late-night pass.

Is there anything we need to say sorry to God about before we say please?

Very often we can only see our prayers answered in hindsight. In unexpected ways or timescales. And answered in the context of God's agenda, not our own.

All of which is a good incentive to be persistent in prayer.

Both Ivan and Mike can look back on lots of rapidly answered prayers. That gives us confidence in prayer. It gives us the motivation to pray, too.

But there have also been plenty of times when we have not witnessed an answer to our prayers, at least in the timeframe or in the way we imagined.

We then have to work very hard not to blame ourselves, or God, for that. We have to remind ourselves to have faith that the prayer has been or will be answered but maybe in a way we cannot see or comprehend.

We have also realized that there is another reason why we may not get the answer to our prayer.

Maybe we are being too self-centered. Not selfish, but self-centric. Jesus said: "I will give you anything you ask for in my name." Have we considered our prayer from God's perspective?

Maybe, just maybe, we've asked for something that isn't good for us or runs counter to God's plans. And who are we to question the validity of those plans?

Jesus was very clear about the power of prayer. But he was also very clear that prayer is not a slot machine. *Request in, answer out.* It requires real effort and perseverance on our part.

In the garden of Gethsemane, Jesus himself prayed the same prayer three times. Luke tells us that he prayed so earnestly that "his sweat was like drops of blood falling to the ground."

Hence this parable.

We can tell you, though, that while some prayers might seem unanswered, we are absolutely certain that there is no such thing as an unheard prayer.

And that is as good a reason as any to be persistent.

Reflection and prayer | In whose name am I praying?

. . . .

_____

_____

_____

_____

_____

What's this story saying to me, here and now?

. . . .

_____

_____

_____

_____

_____

SPARRING ON
THE STUMP

A realtor and a pawnbroker go head-to-head...in a town hall slugfest. Who lands the KO?

"Well, it's continuing to be a beauty of a morning here in downtown sunny Sacramento. I'm Don Jennings and thanks for being with us on KFBK Morning News.

"Now it's time for our 60-second Sound-Off, a minute-long popularity-pleading slug fest.

"The mayoral election happens in just a couple of weeks, so tonight we hear from two of our leading candidates.

First up will be Rafael Martinez, one of our most successful local businesspeople. It feels like half of Sacramento has been bought and sold through his real estate agency.

And following him, Ravi Kapoor, owner of Sacramento's largest chain of pawnbrokers, running for office for the first time.

"Remember the golden rule guys: 90 seconds max, so make it count.

"Rafael, let's have you first."

My record speaks for itself. I'm honest, trustworthy, and fair dealing. My word is my bond. I've set up real estate shops all over Sacramento. I'm sure you've seen our TV commercials and billboards on the highway. If you want to move to a nice neighbor-

selling prized possessions to put food on the table. Nowadays, all our stores offer free financial counseling. We help customers learn how to budget and help them to apply for better jobs. We don't get to go to glitzy parties, but we are invited to the best ones. We celebrate every time someone gets out of debt. We celebrate when we lose customers at the pawnbrokers and gain them at our credit unions. I've never run for office before, but it strikes me that our city could use this kind of help.

hood, you'll find I'm the best in the business. I'm not at all like the other sharks in my trade and certainly not like this greedy pawnbroker, whose main aim is to get his hands on your money. He'll rip you off and kick you when you're down. Check me out on Google: I give loads to charity. I sponsor the polo club, the theater, and the golf club. I move in circles of the up-and-coming. The pawnbroker only knows the down-and-outs. I can make things happen. Vote for me. You'll have a proven winner as your Mayor.

"OK Rafael, thanks. Ravi, your turn."

Being a pawnbroker isn't glamorous. We have a bad rep. When I opened my first shop, I made a killing. But as I started to really listen to my customers, I couldn't live with myself any longer. I met honest people at their most desperate times, selling wedding rings to pay down unpayable medical bills and

"Thanks guys. Now, let's take a look at the online feedback.

"Well, it looks like Ravi is the clear winner tonight. Roll on the election!"

"Next up we have the new Sacramento Kings head coach telling us how he's definitely going to take them to the Finals this season...."

The parable of the Pharisee and the tax collector

Luke 18:9-14

[9]To some who were confident of their own righteousness and looked down on everyone else, Jesus told this parable: [10]"Two men went up to the temple to pray, one a Pharisee and the other a tax collector. [11]The Pharisee stood by himself and prayed:

'God, I thank you that I am not like other people—robbers, evildoers, adulterers—or even like this tax collector. [12]I fast twice a week and give a tenth of all I get.'

[13]"But the tax collector stood at a distance. He would not even look up to heaven, but beat his breast and said, 'God, have mercy on me, a sinner.'

[14]"I tell you that this man, rather than the other, went home justified before God. For all those who exalt themselves will be humbled, and those who humble themselves will be exalted."

So, what's this story saying to US, here and now?

This story cuts straight to the heart of the nature of our attitudes to, and relationships with, other people.

We live in an era of self-sufficiency. From an early age, we are taught the importance of standing on our own two feet, to be confident and assertive. Our abilities are regularly tested at school and the results held up for all to see. Under-performance is not permissible. Poor exam results reflect upon both pupil and teacher.

Successful sportspeople, entrepreneurs and entertainers are held up as role models.

Self-belief is seen as the key to such success.

The problem comes when self-belief turns to belief in self.

When we start believing our own publicity, when we become seduced by our own infallibility, when we become arrogant towards, and dismissive of, those around us, we fail as followers of Jesus.

In the original parable, it is likely that neither the Pharisee nor the tax collector were particularly popular people. The former was typically religiously arrogant, and the latter would probably have cheated his neighbors.

In a similar fashion, neither real estate agents nor pawnbrokers top our public popularity charts, a reflection on the perceptions of the professions rather than the people involved, we hasten to add!

Here we have representatives of each profession seeking to become politicians, another profession that struggles to win public affection.

But we see a marked difference in the attitudes between Rafael and Ravi. One projects self and puts others down; the other espouses service and mutuality. We know who would get our vote.

Elsewhere in the Bible, Jesus was very clear that, before we criticize others, we need to take a long hard look at ourselves. Planks in the eye and all that.

In many ways, we are defined by the nature of our relationships with other people.

This is how we create our true legacy.

Reflection and prayer | Is there a plank in my eye?

. . . .

_____

_____

_____

_____

_____

What's this story saying to **me,** here and now?

. . . .

_____

_____

_____

_____

_____

_____

THE STORE MANAGERS

A hard-nosed boss...gives his lieutenants a chance. Will they step up?

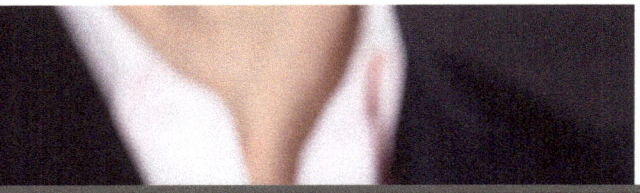

Bart Marinello was a shrewd and successful retailer.

Hard dealing but fair, he had started his first computer supplies shop in Little Rock, Arkansas in 1998, capitalizing upon the rapidly growing interest in the internet and computing in general.

An outstandingly successful first couple of years was followed by two of famine as the dotcom boom turned so spectacularly to bust. For a while, Bart's business looked set to follow so many others into Chapter 11. But Bart was a fighter. Street-fighting retail tactics helped him weather the storm.

By 2004 the business was back on track, and Bart had opened another two stores. His experiences of the early years had not left him, however, and he was known for his cautious and hard-nosed approach to business, judiciously balancing risk and reward.

Then, a year later, disaster struck again but of a very different form than five years earlier. Bart was diagnosed with cancer. There was a ray of light. The doctors were optimistic about Bart's chances. However, he would require surgery followed by an extended period of complete rest.

Bart's fighting spirit roared into action. He summoned his three store managers and gave each autonomous control over their stores. Then, after a successful surgical procedure, he followed the doctors' advice and moved to Hawaii for a year to rest. The managers were instructed to run their stores as if they were their own businesses and under no circumstances to contact Bart.

Two of the managers embraced the opportunity enthusiastically. This was their chance to shine.

Maria launched a laptop repair service which was an immediate success. Ethan trimmed his range, cut his costs, and lowered his prices. This also reaped immediate rewards.

In contrast, the third manager, Jack, was worried. "The boss will be furious if anything goes wrong," he said to himself. "Best to play things safe." And so, he changed nothing. And so, nothing changed.

After his year's sabbatical, Bart returned. Full of vim and vigor. And a sense of his own mortality had spurred in him a desire to do more of what he was good at while he was still able to do so. He set out to open more shops.

So, he called his three managers together.

"Ok guys, let's see where we're at."

Immediately Maria pushed forward. "The laptop repair service was a real winner, boss. The business has rocketed. It's five times bigger."

"That's fantastic, Maria," Bart replied. "I always wanted to do that but didn't have the techie know-how. I'm giving you a 25% stake in the business, and I want you to implement the repair service across all shops."

Ethan then chipped in. "I don't have Maria's technical expertise, she's way ahead of me on that, but I do know the benefit of focusing on the best-selling lines. Profits have doubled."

"You're so right, Ethan. Focus is everything," said Bart. "You'll have a 10% stake and become our Operations Manager across the whole business."

The spotlight fell upon Jack. "Mr. Marinello, I know you are a hard-nosed businessman who will not accept failure. So, I thought it would be best to play it safe. The store is just as you left it."

Bart snapped back. "Being hard-nosed doesn't make me hard-hearted. But in your case, I'm going to make an exception. You should at least have raised prices in line with inflation. And you should have bought in a stock of the newer technology. Your store completely missed out on the tablet market.

"Maria, take Jack's store and convert it into a central base for the laptop repair service.

"Jack, there's no place in this business for those not looking to face the risks involved in growth. I want your desk cleared and you gone within the hour."

The parable of the talents

Matthew 25:14-30

¹⁴ "Again, it will be like a man going on a journey, who called his servants and entrusted his wealth to them. ¹⁵To one he gave five bags of gold, to another two bags, and to another one bag, each according to his ability. Then he went on his journey. ¹⁶The man who had received five bags of gold went at once and put his money to work and gained five bags more. ¹⁷So also, the one with two bags of gold gained two more. ¹⁸But the man who had received one bag went off, dug a hole in the ground and hid his master's money.

¹⁹ "After a long time the master of those servants returned and settled accounts with them. ²⁰The man who had received five bags of gold brought the other five. 'Master,' he said, 'you entrusted me with five bags of gold. See, I have gained five more.'

²¹ "His master replied, 'Well done, good and faithful servant! You have been faithful with a few things; I will put you in charge of many things. Come and share your master's happiness!'

²² "The man with two bags of gold also came. 'Master,' he said, 'you entrusted me with two bags of gold; see, I have gained two more.'

²³ "His master replied, 'Well done, good and faithful servant! You have been faithful with a few things; I will put you in charge of many things. Come and share your master's happiness!'

²⁴ "Then the man who had received one bag of gold came. 'Master,' he said, 'I knew that you are a hard man, harvesting where you have not sown and gathering where you have not scattered seed. ²⁵So I was afraid and went out and hid your gold in the ground. See, here is what belongs to you.'

²⁶ "His master replied, 'You wicked, lazy servant! So you knew that I harvest where I have not sown and gather where I have not scattered seed? ²⁷Well then, you should have put my money on deposit with the bankers, so that when I returned I would have received it back with interest.

²⁸ " 'So take the bag of gold from him and give it to the one who has ten bags. ²⁹For whoever has will be given more, and they will have an abundance. Whoever does not have, even what they have will be taken from them. ³⁰And throw that worthless servant outside, into the darkness, where there will be weeping and gnashing of teeth.'

The parable of the ten minas

Luke
19:11-27

11While they were listening to this, he went on to tell them a parable, because he was near Jerusalem and the people thought that the kingdom of God was going to appear at once. 12He said: "A man of noble birth went to a distant country to have himself appointed king and then to return. 13So he called ten of his servants and gave them ten minas. 'Put this money to work,' he said, 'until I come back.'

14"But his subjects hated him and sent a delegation after him to say, 'We don't want this man to be our king.'

15"He was made king, however, and returned home. Then he sent for the servants to whom he had given the money, in order to find out what they had gained with it.

16"The first one came and said, 'Sir, your mina has earned ten more.'

17"'Well done, my good servant!' his master replied. 'Because you have been trustworthy in a very small matter, take charge of ten cities.'

18"The second came and said, 'Sir, your mina has earned five more.'

19"His master answered, 'You take charge of five cities.'

20"Then another servant came and said, 'Sir, here is your mina; I have kept it laid away in a piece of cloth. 21I was afraid of you, because you are a hard man. You take out what you did not put in and reap what you did not sow.'

22"His master replied, 'I will judge you by your own words, you wicked servant! You knew, did you, that I am a hard man, taking out what I did not put in, and reaping what I did not sow? 23Why then didn't you put my money on deposit, so that when I came back, I could have collected it with interest?'

24"Then he said to those standing by, 'Take his mina away from him and give it to the one who has ten minas.'

25"'Sir,' they said, 'he already has ten!'

26"He replied, 'I tell you that to everyone who has, more will be given, but as for the one who has nothing, even what they have will be taken away. 27But those enemies of mine who did not want me to be king over them—bring them here and kill them in front of me.'"

So, what's this story saying to US, here and now?

At the time of the telling of this parable, Jesus was on the road towards Jerusalem, toward his crucifixion, and at the end of his time with his disciples.

So, his teaching was becoming ever more urgent.

Ivan preached on this parable one Pentecost, so obviously the focus of his preaching would be the Holy Spirit.

While preparing his talk, he became very aware that the talents that Jesus was talking about in this story were the gifts that we receive from the Holy Spirit.

He also became aware that, while the parable urges us to use the gifts we are given, it doesn't say how, which is why it features three different men with bags of gold, three store managers with different skills and stores.

Maybe it's also because there are many different gifts given by the Holy Spirit, given to many different people, and given to use in many different ways.

It's up to each of us to ask the Lord how we can best use the gifts he has given to us.

It's pretty important that we do.

In his sermon, Ivan gave his opinion that the central thrust of this parable was summed up in verse 29 of Matthew's account: "For whoever has will be given more, and they will have an abundance. Whoever does not have, even what they have will be taken from them."

In today's parlance that would translate as: "Use it or lose it."

Wow! Taken in the context of the gifts of the Holy Spirit, that's pretty dramatic, isn't it? There is little that is more urgent for us to comprehend.

The thing is, each one of us has been given gifts that God wants us to use to further his plans. From hospitality and encouragement to prophecy and preaching, from cookery and gardening to writing and arithmetic. Every gift can be supercharged when we make room for the Spirit to get involved.

Sometimes the gift is obvious. Sometimes it's not obvious to us but is to others.

So, our task is twofold. To discern what our gifting is, and then to discern how God wants us to use it.

To best illustrate these last two points, when Mike came to preach on the talents, he found himself telling his own parable.

He's a Brit and so was his audience, so the story is set in an English public school in the south of England and revolves around that really arcane game that the Brits love so much: cricket. (Baseball is its American equivalent, so for "bowler" read pitcher and for "wicketkeeper" read catcher.) We've kept it in its original setting, but don't panic. You don't need to be fluent in cricket to get the point of the story!

The bishop's tale

DISCLAIMER: this is a story of our own invention, not one based upon any of the parables told by Jesus. But we think it's worth telling, nevertheless.

A Bishop was addressing a group of juniors and seniors at his local school's speech day and prize-giving.

He had been asked to offer them some career advice.

So, he told this story:

• •

King Edward VI Grammar School in Southampton is justifiably proud of its cricketing heritage.

They are regular winners of the Hampshire county competition and eleven times national champions.

Their golden era started in 1960 when they discovered three outstanding youngsters in the Year 6 intake, aged 11: Joe, a bowler, Rashid a batter, and Clive, a wicketkeeper/batter.

As the trio progressed through school, the trophies flowed, and they were national champions for four consecutive years.

But in 1967, the boys' time at the school came to an end. Now aged 18, all had done well in their A-level exams, and now they had career choices to make.

Joe had no hesitation in committing himself to cricket. Already on the county's books, he turned full-time professional. At 20 he was selected for England. By his late thirties he had played over 100 tests, 40 of them as captain. He retired on his 40th birthday and joined the BBC's Test Match Special commentary team.

Rashid decided to go into journalism. Starting with the *Southampton Echo*, he was able to continue his cricket at club and county level. He was tipped to join his friend Joe on the England team, but instead he accepted the position as cricket correspondent for the *Daily Telegraph*. His journalistic career flourished and, aged 37, he became the youngest ever Sports Editor of the *Daily Mail*.

Clive was offered a place at Christ Church College, Oxford to read law. Graduating with a First, he became a lawyer and, at the unprecedented age of 32, became a Queens Council and then a High Court judge. He still found the time to play club cricket and, on being voted President of his club, sponsored the establishment of a youth academy which went on to produce two England test players.

• •

After he had finished telling this story, the Bishop's first question was this: "Which of the three made the most of his natural gift for cricket?"

Quickly the answer came back from the students: "Joe."

"You have answered correctly," the Bishop responded.

His second question was this: "Which of the three made the most of his life?"

There was a hubbub of conversation and heated debate, at the end of which the Head Boy rose to his feet: "We don't know."

"Indeed," said the Bishop, "that's not so easy, is it? The answer is that they all did, but they made different life choices. They used their cricketing gift differently, but they did indeed each use it."

Later that evening at dinner, the Bishop found himself sitting next to Canon Peter Thompson, the Head of Divinity at the school.

"I have a question for you, Bishop. Christians have received the gift of the Holy Spirit. How would you advise them to use that?"

The Bishop set down his glass, bowed his head, and thought carefully before responding in a reflective manner.

"That my dear Peter," he said gravely, "is an exceedingly good question, maybe indeed life's most important question.

"Yes, all Christians have the gift of the Holy Spirit, freely given, with no strings attached. But that gift must be opened and used, and it is up to each of us to decide how to do so.

"Many Christians, perhaps indeed most, just get on with their lives, simply trusting in the Spirit and knowing that salvation is secure. There is no sin in this, although they may miss out on some of the riches on offer, much like a talented soprano deciding not to join a choir. My advice to them: that's fine but try to allow the Spirit to work freely in your life.

"Some will combine it with other life choices. A teacher may also become a lay preacher; a successful businessperson may be a philanthropist; or a marketing consultant may help a Christian charity. To them I say, well done, but make sure to seek out and rely on the Spirit in all you do.

"And a few will dedicate their working lives to letting the Holy Spirit work in and through them, becoming ministers, missionaries, or doing other types of vocational Christian work. And my word to them is this: you have chosen the hard and narrow path so always seek to grow further in the Spirit."

The Bishop paused, sipped his drink, and looked directly at Peter.

"The important thing is that, as Christians, we should always acknowledge, accept, and act on the Holy Spirit's presence and gifting in our lives."

Then he added with a rueful smile, "And it may also be that we change our life choice as time goes by. Indeed, I myself used to be an executive for a well-known international petroleum company...."

Reflection and prayer | Am I using my gifts?

What's this story saying to **me,** here and now?

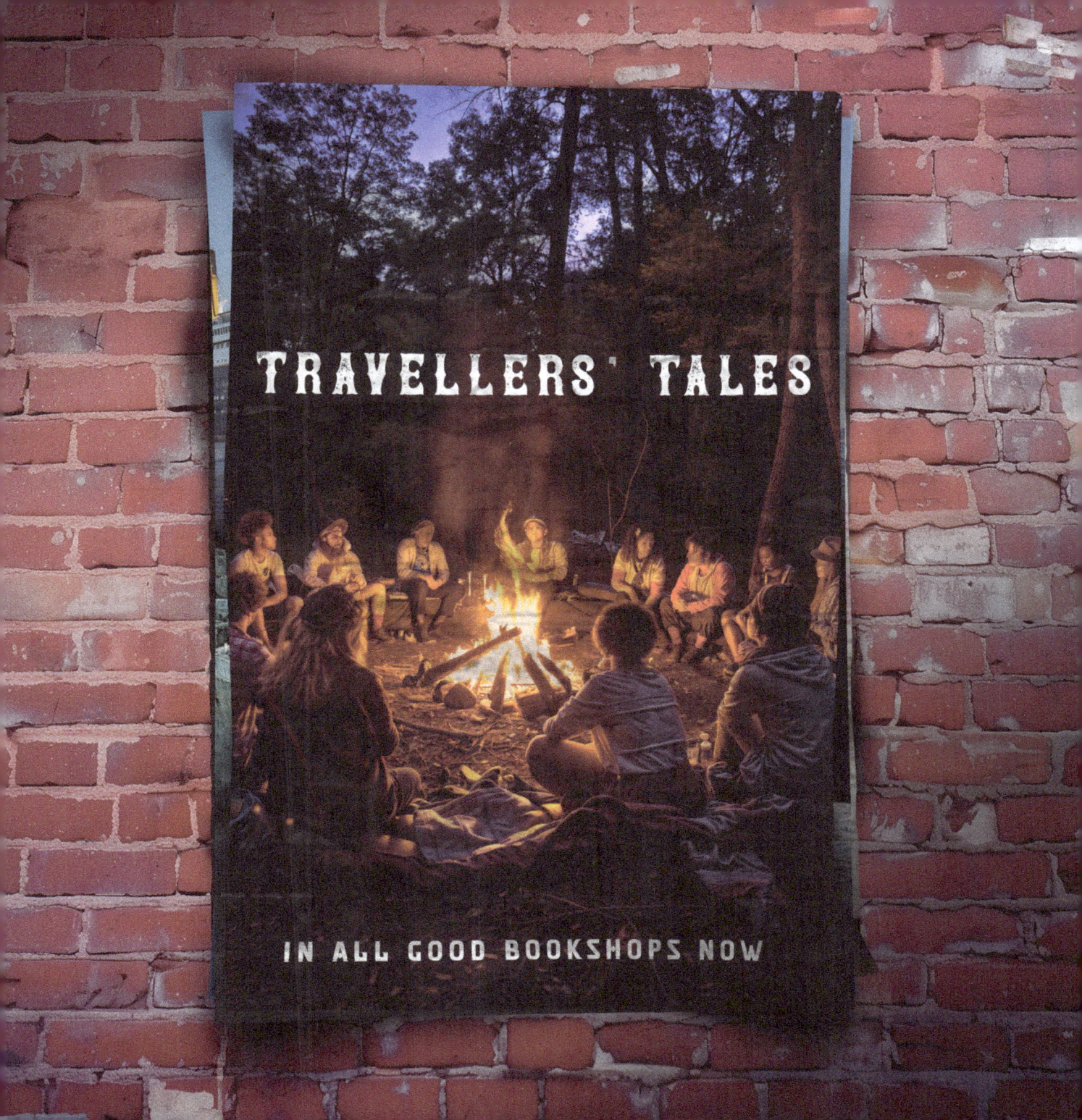

Wow!

These stories really do have bite, don't they.

Do it. (Just) do it.

Do it today because one day tomorrow won't come.

It's never too late to do it, until it is.

Keep doing it.

Do it or lose it.

To the religious authorities, the most shocking was almost certainly the story of the Pharisee and the Tax Collector.

A story that cut to the heart of religious pomposity and hypocrisy.

Do it like you mean it. And if you don't mean it, don't do it.

Just don't.

The stage was set for the final and most compelling stories Jesus would ever tell.

Meek and mild?

Nah!

At this point in his ministerial journey, Jesus reached Jerusalem.

The point at which the spiritual world stood face to face with the physical and material.

When Jesus made his triumphal entry into the city on Palm Sunday, the first thing he did was to throw the money-lenders and traders out of the Temple.

This did not endear him to the authorities.

They were even less impressed when Jesus began teaching and healing in the Temple.

The problem was that people seemed to like him.

So, the authorities challenged him by asking him on what authority he acted. Jesus' reply was an absolute master-stroke. You can read it in Matthew 21: 23-27:

> Jesus entered the temple courts, and, while he was teaching, the chief priests and the elders of the people came to him. "By what authority are you doing these things?" they asked. "And who gave you this authority?"
>
> Jesus replied, "I will also ask you one question. If you answer me, I will tell you by what authority I am doing these things. John's baptism—where did it come from? Was it from heaven, or of human origin?"
>
> They discussed it among themselves and said, "If we say, 'From heaven,' he will ask, 'Then why didn't you believe him?' But if we say, 'Of human origin'—we are afraid of the people, for they all hold that John was a prophet."
>
> So they answered Jesus, "We don't know."
>
> Then he said, "Neither will I tell you by what authority I am doing these things."

Jesus pressed home his advantage with the following three parables, each one a thinly disguised attack upon the Jewish authorities and religious leaders.

Those authorities knew exactly what Jesus was doing but were unable to stop him because of his popularity with the crowds. How they must have seethed and inwardly raged. But there was nothing else they could do. For now…

One over-promised...the other under-promised. But who delivered?

Jesus started his attack with this story:

. . . .

Here's something I want you to really think about.

Kevin and Janice were not happy.

It was the morning of February 5th, the coldest day of the winter thus far in Ashburn, Virginia.

And their boiler had just expired.

There was one bright spot on their horizon.

They had two sons, and both were plumbers.

Kevin called his elder son, Patrick, first.

"I'm so sorry Dad, but I'm in the middle of a big installation, and there's no way I can get around today."

"OK, no sweat Patrick, I'll call Brian."

He had more luck this time.

"No problem. I'm just finishing up a boiler service, so I'll be with you this afternoon," he said.

Come five o'clock, Kevin and Janice were still shivering.

No sign of Brian, and no answer from his mobile.

Kevin did get to leave an irate voicemail.

Just as Kevin hung up, Patrick's van pulled up outside the house.

"Hey, Dad. I felt bad about letting you down, so I've just popped around to see if Brian needs a hand."

An hour later the boiler was up and running again.

The question is simply this: who did what his dad wanted, Patrick or Brian?

"Patrick," came the reply.

The parable of the two sons

Matthew
21:28-32

28"What do you think? There was a man who had two sons. He went to the first and said, 'Son, go and work today in the vineyard.'

29"'I will not,' he answered, but later he changed his mind and went.

30"Then the father went to the other son and said the same thing. He answered, 'I will, sir,' but he did not go.

31"Which of the two did what his father wanted?"

"The first," they answered.

Jesus said to them, "Truly I tell you, the tax collectors and the prostitutes are entering the kingdom of God ahead of you. 32For John came to you to show you the way of righteousness, and you did not believe him, but the tax collectors and the prostitutes did. And even after you saw this, you did not repent and believe him."

So, what's this story saying to **US,** here and now?

These three stories are a little different in that they were aimed very specifically at a certain group of people: the chief priests and the elders of the people. A group that Jesus regarded as being, at best, complacent or worse, hypocritical.

But that doesn't mean that the stories have nothing to say to us, here and now.

We're not told why Brian didn't turn up to mend the boiler, or why the son failed to go and work in the vineyard.

Nor are we told why their respective brothers changed their minds.

The reasons are not important. What is important is that actions speak louder than words.

John the Baptist was widely respected as a prophet, bearing the word of God. A strong call to everyone to repent. To own up to any spiritual shortcomings, to say sorry to God, and to make a real effort to change.

Jesus' shocking message to the chief priests and the elders was that they were spiritually outranked by two of the most despised elements of society: tax collectors and prostitutes. Why? Simply because those people had heard John and acted on his message, whereas the priests had heard but, for whatever reason, not acted.

An old adage says that Jesus came to comfort the disturbed and to disturb the comfortable.

That is as true today as it was then. It's all too easy to become a little too comfortable in one's faith, to be long on good intentions and short on practical actions.

Reflection and prayer | Do my good intentions result in good actions?

. . . .

_____

_____

_____

_____

_____

What's this story saying to **me,** here and now?

. . . .

_____

_____

_____

_____

_____

_____

THE REBELLIOUS
BOARD

BY DESIGN

Amy signs over her 'baby'...
but her choice of 'parents' sucks.
What's she gonna do?

Jesus continued his attack on the authorities by telling this very pointed story, which greatly angered them:

• •

Amy Jackson founded and built up a highly successful design company in Vancouver that worked for many blue-chip retailers and manufacturers. It had made her a millionaire several times over. She then got a hankering to turn her talents to the publishing business in the USA.

She struck an arrangement with the directors of the company, which involved selling them 25% of the business with options to buy a further 50% over time. She would remove herself from the operational side of the company and step down from the Board to become a sleeping investor. The company would belong to her former directors and employees to do with as they wished.

So, she headed south to Seattle where her blend of warm humanity coated by an assertive, armor-plated business acumen made her a huge success.

Back in the design company, things were not so sweet and light. Sure, it continued to be successful. Indeed, it grew. But the culture had changed, particularly in the way it treated its staff. The directors became greedy. Bonuses were withheld, staffing levels reduced, working hours increased, and salary reviews postponed. Some employees wrote to Amy. Moved by this unrest in her "baby," she asked the directors to amend these practices and keep faith with the staff. They responded by firing the employees who had written to her.

Shocked by this, Amy asked some of her former senior managers she trusted to intercede on her behalf. Aggrieved by this apparent "interference," the directors fired these managers too and then voted to reduce the dividend to external shareholders (i.e. Amy). Feeling this to be a breach of company law, Amy exercised the right she had retained to appoint a Non-Executive Director to the Board of the company to represent her interests. She sent her son in this capacity, feeling that he would command more respect than an unknown outsider. Not at all deterred by this, the other directors immediately voted him off the Board.

At this point, Amy's patience ran out. She returned to Vancouver, called an extraordinary shareholders' meeting, re-assumed direct day-to-day control of the company, fired the entire Board, and appointed a whole new set of directors to run the business.

The parable of the tenants

Matthew
21:33-46

^{33}"Listen to another parable: There was a landowner who planted a vineyard. He put a wall around it, dug a winepress in it and built a watchtower. Then he rented the vineyard to some farmers and moved to another place. ^{34}When the harvest time approached, he sent his servants to the tenants to collect his fruit.

^{35}"The tenants seized his servants; they beat one, killed another, and stoned a third. ^{36}Then he sent other servants to them, more than the first time, and the tenants treated them the same way. ^{37}Last of all, he sent his son to them. 'They will respect my son,' he said.

^{38}"But when the tenants saw the son, they said to each other, 'This is the heir. Come, let's kill him and take his inheritance.' ^{39}So they took him and threw him out of the vineyard and killed him.

^{40}"Therefore, when the owner of the vineyard comes, what will he do to those tenants?"

^{41}"He will bring those wretches to a wretched end," they replied, "and he will rent the vineyard to other tenants, who will give him his share of the crop at harvest time."

^{42}Jesus said to them, "Have you never read in the Scriptures:

"'The stone the builders rejected has become the cornerstone; the Lord has done this, and it is marvelous in our eyes'?

^{43}"Therefore I tell you that the kingdom of God will be taken away from you and given to a people who will produce its fruit. ^{44}Anyone who falls on this stone will be broken to pieces; anyone on whom it falls will be crushed."

^{45}When the chief priests and the Pharisees heard Jesus' parables, they knew he was talking about them. ^{46}They looked for a way to arrest him, but they were afraid of the crowd because the people held that he was a prophet.

Mark 12:1-12

¹Jesus then began to speak to them in parables: "A man planted a vineyard. He put a wall around it, dug a pit for the winepress and built a watchtower. Then he rented the vineyard to some farmers and moved to another place. ²At harvest time he sent a servant to the tenants to collect from them some of the fruit of the vineyard. ³But they seized him, beat him and sent him away empty-handed. ⁴Then he sent another servant to them; they struck this man on the head and treated him shamefully. ⁵He sent still another, and that one they killed. He sent many others; some of them they beat, others they killed.

⁶"He had one left to send, a son, whom he loved. He sent him last of all, saying, 'They will respect my son.'

⁷"But the tenants said to one another, 'This is the heir. Come, let's kill him, and the inheritance will be ours.' ⁸So they took him and killed him, and threw him out of the vineyard.

⁹"What then will the owner of the vineyard do? He will come and kill those tenants and give the vineyard to others. ¹⁰Haven't you read this passage of Scripture:

"'The stone the builders rejected has become the cornerstone; ¹¹the Lord has done this, and it is marvelous in our eyes'?"

¹²Then the chief priests, the teachers of the law and the elders looked for a way to arrest him because they knew he had spoken the parable against them. But they were afraid of the crowd; so they left him and went away.

Luke 20:9-19

⁹He went on to tell the people this parable: "A man planted a vineyard, rented it to some farmers and went away for a long time. ¹⁰At harvest time he sent a servant to the tenants so they would give him some of the fruit of the vineyard. But the tenants beat him and sent him away empty-handed. ¹¹He sent another servant, but that one also they beat and treated shamefully and sent away empty-handed. ¹²He sent still a third, and they wounded him and threw him out.

¹³"Then the owner of the vineyard said, 'What shall I do? I will send my son, whom I love; perhaps they will respect him.'

¹⁴"But when the tenants saw him, they talked the matter over. 'This is the heir,' they said. 'Let's kill him, and the inheritance will be ours.' ¹⁵So they threw him out of the vineyard and killed him.

"What then will the owner of the vineyard do to them? ¹⁶He will come and kill those tenants and give the vineyard to others."

When the people heard this, they said, "God forbid!"

¹⁷Jesus looked directly at them and asked, "Then what is the meaning of that which is written:

"'The stone the builders rejected has become the cornerstone'? ¹⁸Everyone who falls on that stone will be broken to pieces; anyone on whom it falls will be crushed."

¹⁹The teachers of the law and the chief priests looked for a way to arrest him immediately, because they knew he had spoken this parable against them. But they were afraid of the people.

So, what's this story saying to US, here and now?

The ante was being upped. The authorities now were being accused not only of ignoring God's word but intimidating, punishing, and even killing those who had brought it to them.

There was a historical basis for this. The Old Testament prophets had suffered greatly at the hands of the authorities. Some prophets had been killed by them.

Jesus angered the authorities further by claiming that he was God's son and that they would kill him too. Which, of course, they did.

But what has this altercation got to do with us?

The priests were motivated by two things: a desire to protect their position and to project their worldview: protect and project.

We see the pattern repeated throughout our society today, in governments, political parties, commercial corporations, powerful individuals, and even in church streams.

We hold our (political/social/commercial/individual/spiritual/theological) belief and worldview to be uniquely correct. It's the way we think, and we don't want it challenged; and we believe you should think that way too. And, if need be, we'll make you.

Protect and project.

It seems to be endemic to the human race.

As such, each one of us individually may not be wholly untainted.

We may not have intimidated, harmed, or killed in a physical sense, but there may have been times when we have done so verbally to defend our own position or to enforce our point of view.

Perhaps we may have done so directly, bullying, or maybe indirectly, behind someone's back, gossiping and undermining.

Over the years, we may have been guilty on both counts.

Either way, we may have been hurtful, not merciful.

Protect and project.

The only thing that Jesus seeks to protect is us. The only thing he projects is love.

Reflection and prayer | Have I ever been hurtful?

· ·

What's this story saying to **me,** here and now?

· ·

THE BIG GAME

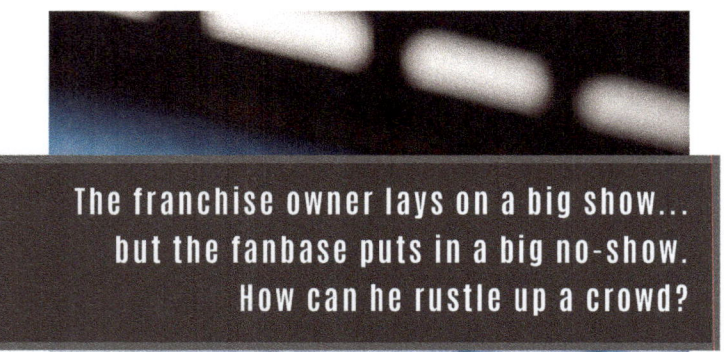

The franchise owner lays on a big show...
but the fanbase puts in a big no-show.
How can he rustle up a crowd?

The third story hammered home the last part of Jesus' attack:

· ·

In the late 1950s the Midgley family—John, Jean, and their 3-year-old toddler Gordon—relocated from Pittsburgh to Leeds, England. It was a good move. John, an engineer, set up a business that boomed.

His only regret was not being able to actively follow his beloved Steelers, a regret compounded when young Gordon fell in love with soccer. Really?

But, come 1962, little Gordon was thrilled when his local amateur team, the Frimley Rangers, made it all the way through to the quarter-finals of the nationally prestigious FA Cup. Their opponents would be the mighty Manchester United.

Gordon was there at the game, perched on his Dad's shoulders, draped in his green and white scarf, cheering himself hoarse and loving every second of it. No matter that they were then blasted apart, 9-1, they had tweaked the noses of the big boys and put Frimley on the map.

Little Gordon (or increasingly big Gordon as he took over his Dad's business and grew in wealth, importance, and weight) never forgot the thrill of that cup run, and in 2002, some forty years later, he bought the club. Over the next few years, "King Gordon," as he was known, put a lot of money into the club to bring in players and upgrade its facilities.

Imagine then Gordon's delight as, in the 2010 season, the Frimley Rangers made it through to the FA Cup Third Round, the point at which the big Premier League clubs entered the competition. Would history repeat itself? Would they draw Manchester United again? Could they change history and win—or at the very least score twice—this time?

Despite all the improvements, the ground could still only hold 5,000, and there was talk of moving the venue should Frimley draw one of the big clubs. But Gordon was having absolutely none of it. "If we're drawn at home we'll be playing here. The fans will just have to diet," which was rich coming from the 250 lb Gordon.

Tension during the draw was extreme. Frimley were seventh to be drawn—at home!

"YES!" yelled Gordon, "and United are still to be drawn!" United were indeed the next team to be drawn, but not, unfortunately, the Manchester variety of United. Frimley's opposition would be Hyde United, the only other amateur team left in the cup.

Disappointment turned to despair as neighboring Barnsley drew Manchester United at home.

But Gordon had not survived and prospered during his 45 years of life in Frimley by falling at first hurdles. "The party's still on," he boomed. "We'll just have to give Hyde a good hiding—ha ha ha."

So, the plans for the game and the associated festivities progressed and the great day dawned. With a full house of 5,000 in prospect Gordon was at the ground bright and early.

But an hour before kick-off there was hardly a soul around.

Gordon sent some ground stewards into the town to chivvy people up, but they came back puzzled. "They don't seem to be coming," they said. "Don't be silly, of course they'll be coming," yelled Gordon. "Just get back there and tell them to get their backsides in gear and get along here because I've got 5,000 quality burgers for free, good beer, a rock band and the Frimley Frantic Freefall parachute team dropping by in 45 minutes."

The hapless stewards returned to the by now deserted streets of Frimley to deliver King Gordon's invitation. It became apparent that streets were deserted because a good proportion of the male population of Frimley, including just about all those who had bought tickets for the big game, had now instead decided to head off to Barnsley to see them play the other United. Two stewards tried to remonstrate with one group of fans who were on their way to the bus station but were beaten up for their pains.

Gordon was apoplectic. "Right, the heck with them!" Just go back into town and say to anyone you find that they'll be welcome here. Anyone. Male, female, octogenarian, teenager, suckling babe, Frimley born, or on a two-week heritage tour from Colombia. Just tell them we'd appreciate their support and can promise them a good time."

And that's what happened. The ground slowly filled up and by the time of kickoff was a sea of green and white.

Gordon himself, restored to his normal indomitable good humor, roamed the ground soaking up the atmosphere, cracking jokes, and leading the communal singing. He reflected that these were truly the salt of Frimley, people that really appreciated the local community and this unexpected opportunity to pull together and support it.

But then he ran into a man not wearing an inch of green or white, burping free burgers and quite obviously one or two pints of the specially brewed local ale to the worse. "My friend," cooed Gordon (and those who knew Gordon also knew that when he cooed it was time to check the location of the nearest nuclear fall-out shelter), "my friend, why are you not draped in the glorious green and white of the all-conquering Frimley Rangers and festooned with rosettes and garlands of the same color?"

The man was speechless (or perhaps just incapable of speech).

"Throw him out," exploded the mercurial Gordon, "or better still throw him in—into the nearest cesspit."

"But, Mr. Midgley," the stewards protested, "you invited him here."

"Of course, I invited him. I invited them all, but that doesn't mean I necessarily choose to let him stay. Now, kick him out and he can spend the rest of his life regretting the day he missed the game of the century."

Epilogue:

Frimley beat Hyde that afternoon.

They also got to meet Manchester United that season, at Wembley, in the Final, in front of 90,000 people.

They scored two goals.

Gordon was delirious.

Sadly, United scored five.

The parable of the wedding banquet

Matthew
22:1-14

¹Jesus spoke to them again in parables, saying: ²"The kingdom of heaven is like a king who prepared a wedding banquet for his son. ³He sent his servants to those who had been invited to the banquet to tell them to come, but they refused to come.

⁴"Then he sent some more servants and said, 'Tell those who have been invited that I have prepared my dinner: My oxen and fattened cattle have been butch-

ered, and everything is ready. Come to the wedding banquet.'

⁵"But they paid no attention and went off—one to his field, another to his business. ⁶The rest seized his servants, mistreated them and killed them. ⁷The king was enraged. He sent his army and destroyed those murderers and burned their city.

⁸"Then he said to his servants, 'The wedding banquet is ready, but those I invited did not deserve to come. ⁹So go to the street corners and invite to the banquet anyone you find.' ¹⁰So the servants went out into the streets and gathered all the people they could find, the bad as well as the good, and the wedding hall was filled with guests.

¹¹"But when the king came in to see the guests, he noticed a man there who was not wearing wedding clothes. ¹²He asked, 'How did you get in here without wedding clothes, friend?' The man was speechless.

¹³"Then the king told the attendants, 'Tie him hand and foot, and throw him outside, into the darkness, where there will be weeping and gnashing of teeth.'

¹⁴"For many are invited, but few are chosen."

So, what's this story saying to US, here and now?

It's a great story, isn't it? And it has a real sting in the tail. It's also one of Jesus' more multi-dimensional parables, providing messaging at many different levels. But the authorities and chief priests were no mugs. They would have understood all the messages, and all were aimed at them.

Try your own hand at hotwiring it. Pray over it and see what emerges. Then meditate upon it. Make sure to use the notes page to jot down your thoughts.

As for us, we're going to follow the KISS principle: keep it simple, stupid, and limit ourselves to four short observations.

First thought. Accept the invitation.

God has invited us, through his son, to a heavenly banquet, to a party where the whole of creation—Heaven and Earth—will be renewed, including us, together with all the believers that have preceded and will succeed us.

There is no better gig. Let's not get seduced by other attractions that are superficially glitzy, but hollow inside. And let's certainly not throw the invite into the trash can.

Second thought. Value the invitation.

Let's make sure we appreciate the uniqueness and the value of the invitation we have been given. Yes, it is given to us for free, but it has enormous face value because it was issued at great cost—Jesus' life.

Third thought. RSVP.

We have the invitation. But we must respond to it. Say "yes," today!

Final thought. Follow the dress code.

And what is that dress code? Jesus.

We need to be clothed in Christ.

Reflection and prayer | Have I accepted the invitation?

· ·

_____

_____

_____

_____

_____

_____

What's this story saying to **me,** here and now?

· ·

_____

_____

_____

_____

_____

_____

By the time Jesus had finished telling these three stories, the authorities were livid. In desperation, they fired three legalistically tricky questions at him, each designed to trap him into a verbal indiscretion (Matthew 22: 15-46). First the Pharisees, then the Sadducees, and then the Pharisees again all questioned him. But Jesus cleverly turned the questions right back on them and finished with a question of his own, which tied them in knots instead.

He then followed up with an astonishing verbal assault, during which he labeled the authorities variously as hypocrites, blind guides, blind fools, whitewashed tombs, and a brood of vipers. He also accused them and their predecessors of betrayal and murder. It's all recorded in Matthew Chapter 23. Do read it.

Jesus would have known exactly what he was doing: forcing the authorities into a corner. "Back me or sack me" in modern parlance. He would have also known the almost inevitable consequences. In the eyes and minds of the authorities, he was just too dangerous to be allowed to stick around. Like the rebellious Board and the vineyard tenants, they had too much to lose, particularly position and power.

Protect and project.

And so, the murderous plot was hatched, which would fulfill the ancient prophecies.

As he neared his crucifixion, it was only natural that Jesus would want to focus on why his physical, mortal, human death was necessary; what it would mean for us; the unique invitation it would create for us to follow him along the path to spiritual, immortal, eternal life; and the harsh consequences for us if we fail to do so.

So, the last three parables he told focused upon his return: the second coming.

Each of these stories, culminating in the chilling depiction of Judgement Day, asks all people, then, now, you and us, and everyone in the time to come, one very direct question: "Where do *you* stand?"

It's the most important question each of us will ever have to answer:

Where do *I* stand?

TALES OF
THE EXPECTED

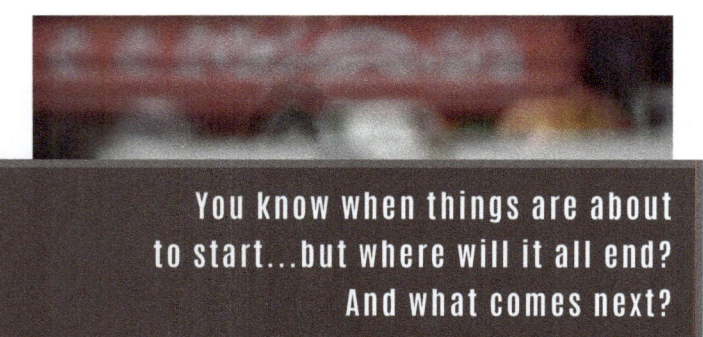

You know when things are about to start...but where will it all end? And what comes next?

Jesus' final three parables start with another typically enigmatic story. Appropriately, it's about the end of the age. We've expanded it into three vignettes:

• •

When the cars move off the line three abreast for the warm-up lap, you know that the rolling start is underway and the Indy 500 is about to roar into action.

If you see the lights dim or hear the bell ring whilst you're in the lobby of the theatre, you know that you have a couple of minutes to get to your seat because the performance is about to commence.

When the official throws the ball in the air for the jump ball, you know for sure that the basketball game action is starting.

THEATRE TICKET

admit one

The parable of the fig tree

Matthew 24:32-35

32"Now learn this lesson from the fig tree: As soon as its twigs get tender and its leaves come out, you know that summer is near. 33Even so, when you see all these things, you know that it is near, right at the door. 34Truly I tell you, this generation will certainly not pass away until all these things have happened. 35Heaven and earth will pass away, but my words will never pass away."

Mark 13:28-31

28"Now learn this lesson from the fig tree: As soon as its twigs get tender and its leaves come out, you know that summer is near. 29Even so, when you see these things happening, you know that it is near, right at the door. 30Truly I tell you, this generation will certainly not pass away until all these things have happened. 31Heaven and earth will pass away, but my words will never pass away."

Luke 21:29-33

29He told them this parable: "Look at the fig tree and all the trees. 30When they sprout leaves, you can see for yourselves and know that summer is near. 31Even so, when you see these things happening, you know that the kingdom of God is near.

32"Truly I tell you, this generation will certainly not pass away until all these things have happened. 33Heaven and earth will pass away, but my words will never pass away."

So, what's this story saying to US, here and now?

Hmm, this is a tricky one. It's clearly an important parable as it's one of just seven recorded by each of Matthew, Mark, and Luke in their biographies of Jesus.

Jesus told the parable in response to some specific questions from his close disciples.

He preceded it by foretelling the destruction of Jerusalem.

Not surprisingly, they were quite keen to know when that might happen.

But then they upped the ante by going on to ask what the sign would be for Jesus' second coming and the end of the age.

Well, if you were sitting in front of the man who had all the answers, you'd probably ask the same things. Ivan and Mike know they would—and a lot more besides.

The trouble is that Jesus, being the frequently enigmatic type that he was, makes it difficult for his listeners to work out which answer was being given to what question.

As a result, theologians and historians have been tying themselves in knots about it ever since.

Which, we like to think, may have been part of Jesus' intention.

But it hasn't got us any closer to answering our own question, has it? So perhaps he has snookered us as well.

For what it's worth, this is our take.

We believe Jesus would have fastened upon the really big question: how will we know when he has truly come again to make all things new?

In response to that, he launches into 28 verses (in Matthew's Gospel) of apocalyptic prophecy. Read these verses. And then try and put yourselves in the position of the disciples once he had finished.

For anyone who has seen the cult movie *Galaxy Quest*, there is a scene that may help.

It's the one where the crew are unexpectedly transported across the galaxy for the first time wrapped only in a kind of transparent, jelly, cling-film, bubble, that, on arrival upon a huge starship, dissolves and leaves them as quivering, speechless wrecks.

If you've seen the movie, we're sure you will agree that helps. If you've not seen the movie, watch it!

So, confronted by his disciples' similarly shocked and stunned expressions, Jesus resorts to something more in line with their everyday experience: the fig tree.

"Look guys, you know summer is about to start when the fig tree gets all buddy. You don't know why you know; you just know. It will be the same with my return. You'll know when you know."

Except that, speaking personally, we wouldn't know a fig tree if it fell on us. We have oak, ash, cherry, horse chestnut, and pine growing around us. But neither of us has a fig tree.

But we do know when the Indianapolis 500 is about to start, when to take our seat at the theatre, and when the basketball game is beginning.

So, we're not going to worry about exactly when Jesus is going to return.

We'll know when we know.

And we'll try to live every day as if it was going to be today, which is what we think Jesus may have really been getting at here, together with the implied question: "Where do you stand?"

Reflection and prayer | What if it were today?

· ·

_____

_____

_____

_____

_____

_____

What's this story saying to me, here and now?

· ·

_____

_____

_____

_____

_____

_____

THE IMPATIENT
PAPARAZZI

A chance for local journos to make their name...but the big networks are trying to cut in. Who gets to break the story?

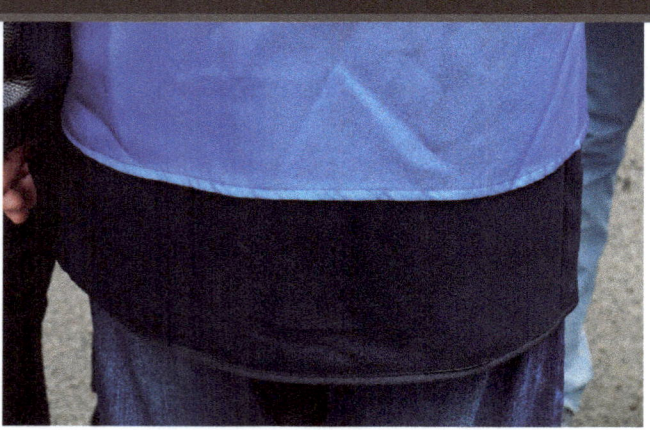

The can of worms had been opened. The end of the age was on the conversational table. Understandably, the disciples were keen to know more about how they might prepare for it, so Jesus told them this story.

• •

Ivan here. Sorry folks but this one is pure Mike. He was on a roll, and I couldn't stop him. Here's a little glossary to help you understand his Britspeak:

Falmouth: a town in Cornwall in SW England. Noted for its wet, cool, climate even in summer, and its lack of mobile phone coverage!

Centre: center, doh!

Media/Press hacks: journalists.

Pasty: a Cornish delicacy. A hand-held pastry filled with meat and vegetables.

Falmouth Packet: a Cornish newspaper.

Jobsworth: someone who puts their job before common sense.

Brollies: slang for umbrellas.

Nat Bulios: you'll have to work that out for yourselves. We couldn't possibly comment!

July 18th: Mike's birthday

Falmouth was buzzing.

Not only did the town have a brand-new sports centre on the outskirts of town, something for which the locals had been screaming for ages, but it was to be officially opened by global athletics superstar Nat Bulios. (A great athlete, but always inclined to get a bit mixed up.)

The big moment was set for 10 am on July 18th.

A typical Cornish summer day dawned—low scudding clouds and driving rain.

The media pack gathered early that morning at the centre. The TV camera crews led the way, setting up at 6:00 am. By 8:00 am, every snack bar in the area had been cleaned out of bacon sandwiches.

The press hacks could afford to be more leisurely and to stay dry a bit longer. They arrived outside the new centre at 9:00 am, just in case there was an early arrival. Although the experienced ones knew there was more likelihood of a delay, particularly as Nat was being driven straight from Heathrow that very day.

And so it proved.

10:00 am came and went with no word on Nat's whereabouts, the lack of information not helped by an absence of a mobile phone signal. (Remember, this is Cornwall.) By noon, the TV boys had to pack up and go. They were scheduled to cover an important address by the Prime Minister in Cardiff later that day.

Then, just before 2:00 pm, word began to spread that Nat would not arrive until at least 5:00 pm, at which point a huge crowd of cold, wet, frustrated, annoyed, but above all, hungry hacks headed back into town to search out pasties and, while there, find a dry place with some landlines to file interim reports to their main news desks.

A few local press journos from the *Falmouth Packet* and the *West Briton* remained. It was July, so local knowledge had given them the foresight to bring umbrellas. They had no main news desk to report to; they were it. They also knew that, in Cornwall, time is a very flexible concept, and, most importantly, and in the spirit of true Cornish people everywhere, they had brought their own pasties with them.

So, they were in exactly the right place when, at 3:00 pm, a stretch limo arrived outside the sports centre and the unmistakable form of the great Nat Bulios unfolded itself from the back seat.

He laughed and performed his famous fake collapse. "Well, this sure is an intimate affair. Already I am loving this place." He then grabbed a few bedraggled schoolchildren and performed his even more famous trademark bow and arrow pose with them. After signing a flurry of soggy autograph books, he went into the sports centre. But the security men stopped the local journos from following. "Sorry guys, the ceremony is reserved for the national TV channels."

Nat himself interceded. "Excuse me? I don't see any TV cameras. I'm running late, so I have to be out of here in an hour. These guys are here, so they get the story. Let them inside."

As the news of Nat's arrival spread around town, the reporters from the national newspapers dropped their pasties and raced back.

As they reached the doors to the centre, the security men once again blocked their path. "Sorry, the ceremony has started and no one else is allowed in."

"Don't give us that, you jobsworths," the angry hacks howled at them. "We're from the big nationals, of course we'll be allowed in."

One of the security men stepped to one side and talked into his radio.

After a couple of minutes, he turned back with a cheerful face. The press pack took a step forward.

"Uh-uh, not so fast people. I'm afraid it's a no-go. Nat says he doesn't care who you are or where you're from. He's given the story to the people who were good enough to be here when he arrived. Now if you'd kindly step outside gents. Oh, I see it's raining again. I hope you have your brollies with you. No? What a shame."

The parable of the ten virgins

Matthew
25:1-13

[1]"At that time the kingdom of heaven will be like ten virgins who took their lamps and went out to meet the bridegroom. [2]Five of them were foolish and five were wise. [3]The foolish ones took their lamps but did not take any oil with them. [4]The wise ones, however, took oil in jars along with their lamps. [5]The bridegroom was a long time in coming, and they all became drowsy and fell asleep.

[6]"At midnight the cry rang out: 'Here's the bridegroom! Come out to meet him!'

[7]"Then all the virgins woke up and trimmed their lamps. [8]The foolish ones said to the wise, 'Give us some of your oil; our lamps are going out.'

[9]"'No,' they replied, 'there may not be enough for both us and you. Instead, go to those who sell oil and buy some for yourselves.'

[10]"But while they were on their way to buy the oil, the bride-groom arrived. The virgins who were ready went in with him to the wedding banquet. And the door was shut.

[11]"Later the others also came. 'Lord, Lord,' they said, 'open the door for us!'

[12]"But he replied, 'Truly I tell you, I don't know you.'

[13]"Therefore keep watch, because you do not know the day or the hour.

So, what's this story saying to US, here and now?

Most of us know the date of our birthday. It forms a crucial part of our personal identity in legal terms.

It's something we use as a cause of celebration once a year.

There are other dates known to us that we also celebrate: a wedding anniversary, Christmas, New Year's Eve, Valentine's Day, Mother's Day, Easter (although that date moves around a bit).

We can prepare properly for these occasions because we know that they are coming.

But a date we don't know with such advanced precision is our "death day."

Our death day may be the most important date of all because that's when we get to meet Jesus and see him more perfectly. Our earthly blinkers will be taken off, and we get to gaze at the one to whom everyone must bow: senators and schoolkids; journalists and jockeys; CEOs and chefs; socialites and social workers; teachers and preachers; drug-dealers and drug-users; pastors and prostitutes. Mike and Ivan, even. And you, dear reader, too.

But because we don't know the date, manner, or circumstances in which we shall leave this world, it's hard to prepare for it in advance, apart from making a will and funeral arrangements that cater for its inevitable arrival, whenever that may be.

Of course, we won't be there to help mark the occasion, not in any active, physical sense anyway!

But we will be there when we meet Jesus.

And we certainly need to be prepared for that.

As we don't know when, where or how, we need to be constantly prepared.

The best way to do this is by staying in a close relationship with him.

That's what this parable is saying to us here and now. It's asking us the question once again: "Where do *you* stand?"

Reflection and prayer | Am I prepared?

· ·

_____

_____

_____

_____

_____

What's this story saying to **me,** here and now?

· ·

_____

_____

_____

_____

_____

A SHANTY OF SAILBOATS AND MOTORBOATS

Judgement is being pronounced...
winners to one side...losers to the other.
Who gets that sinking feeling?

For the avoidance of doubt and confusion amongst those of you who regard a 'shanty' as an old wooden shed, Mike and Ivan refer you to their trusty Merriam-Webster dictionary which gives an additional definition of a 'shanty' as being 'a song sung by sailors in rhythm with their work'.

We thought this would be an appropriate title given the 'salty nature' of this story. For the further avoidance of doubt and confusion, we hasten to add we are using the Merriam-Webster definition of 'salty' as 'smacking of the sea or nautical life'.

Anyway, that's enough definitions, on with the story...

Just as Jesus' first parable mirrored his first miracle, so it is fitting that his last parable should mirror what will be his final action: judgement.

Judgement Day is not the easiest of topics. Here's how Jesus might address it:

· ·

The back of the knife struck the wine glass.

Three times, quickly.

Again.

And again.

By the time the echo of the third set of strikes had rung around the room, the post-dinner conversation had halted, and the 30 pairs of eyes and ears around the U-shaped banqueting table had refocussed upon the immaculately tailored 52-year-old man who had risen from his chair.

Jules Fine was the Founder and Chairman of Fine Communications, the world's third-largest advertising, PR, and marketing communications group and the only group that still remained in private ownership.

Jules was a giant of the industry, a legend. Charisma flowed from him like Vesuvian lava.

"Friends, today marks 25 years since the original Fine & Partners ad agency opened its doors for business.

"The first five years were difficult, to say the least. That you can blame on me for choosing to start a business a year before a global recession, but it gave us an enormous advantage. While others were cutting staff, we were adding them. We became a hothouse for talent and that powered us for the next 15 years.

"Five years ago, the next recession struck. Deeper and more savage than anything the world had seen before. Yet we doubled in size in the first two years, and now I can tell you that we have redoubled.

"As members of our Worldwide Board of Directors, everyone around this table has profited."

As he paused for a sip of water, there was applause around the table and, amongst the American contingent, some high-fives.

"Now I have an important task to perform."

The room instantly quietened and swelled with pregnant expectancy.

"I have been asking myself a question. How sustainable is this success? In the history of mankind, no empire, whether business, political, or military has survived indefinitely. Frequently, the peak of success heralds an imminent decline and fall. Does our recent success mask an awful truth that we may have reached the end of our life cycle?"

The atmosphere in the room changed subtly. The expectancy was shaded with uncertainty. Where was this going?

"Please look at your place cards. You'll have noticed that some are in the shape of sailboats and others of motorboats.

"While this may chime with our surroundings here in Portofino, it is not just a design conceit.

"If you have a sailboat, please come and stand to my right. Everyone with motorboats, come stand to my left."

In puzzlement and with a slight feeling of trepidation, people abandoned their places at the table and gathered in the two groups, 10 to Jules' right and 20 to his left.

Jules turned to his right. "You people have served me well and will continue to do so. You will each receive a year's salary as a bonus in reward."

He then swiveled 180 degrees. "I'm sorry to say that you have not served me as well and that your contracts will be terminated immediately."

Jules sat down as the room exploded. A cocktail of astonishment and shock, mixed and shaken with relief and despair.

After a few minutes, the back of the knife struck the wine glass again.

This time it took five repetitions of the three-strike sequence to bring order to the room.

Jules stayed seated and looked to his right and then to his left.

"I'm guessing you want to know how I reached this decision.

"Well, I'm going to tell you.

"When I founded this company, I had a vision. I wanted my company to be the most admired ad agency in the world, the company that people wanted to work for beyond any other.

"I then decided that the best way, the only way, that vision would be achieved was if we pursued three values in all that we did.

"You all know these values: they should be written on your hearts:

Integrity.

Humility.

Compassion.

"One of my favorite mottos is 'what gets measured gets done.' So, every year, I've conducted research to check out how we perform against these values. I have been the only person ever to see the results of this research.

"For 20 years, we received near perfect scores on all three dimensions. But over the last five years there has been a steady decline.

"So, this year I did some additional research. I asked a cross-section of our staff, our clients, and our suppliers to rate each of you, individually, against our values.

"My reasoning was that each time one of our staff, clients, or suppliers interacted with one of my senior leaders it should be as if they were doing so with me personally."

He stood and faced the people on his left.

"You all fell short, far too short to remain in this company. Your continued presence would undermine all I believe in and have tried so hard to have us achieve. Please leave the room now."

There was an uncomfortable silence and then they started to drift out.

He turned to face those who remained.

"Thank you for staying true to my values and therefore to me. I know I can trust you to take the company forward over the next 25 years. We have most certainly not reached the end of our life cycle. Indeed, if we continue to stay true to our values there will be no life cycle.

"I think a glass of champagne is in order."

The parable of the sheep and the goats

Matthew
25:31-46

31 "When the Son of Man comes in his glory, and all the angels with him, he will sit on his glorious throne. 32All the nations will be gathered before him, and he will separate the people one from another as a shepherd separates the sheep from the goats. 33He will put the sheep on his right and the goats on his left.

34 "Then the King will say to those on his right, 'Come, you who are blessed by my Father; take your inheritance, the kingdom prepared for you since the creation of the world. 35For I was hungry and you gave me something to eat, I was thirsty and you gave me something to drink, I was a stranger and you invited me in, 36I needed clothes and you clothed me, I was sick and you looked after me, I was in prison and you came to visit me.'

37 "Then the righteous will answer him, 'Lord, when did we see you hungry and feed you, or thirsty and give you something to drink? 38When did we see you a stranger and invite you in, or needing clothes and clothe you? 39When did we see you sick or in prison and go to visit you?'

40 "The King will reply, 'Truly I tell you, whatever you did for one of the least of these brothers and sisters of mine, you did for me.'

41 "Then he will say to those on his left, 'Depart from me, you who are cursed, into the eternal fire prepared for the devil and his angels. 42For I was hungry and you gave me nothing to eat, I was thirsty and you gave me nothing to drink, 43I was a stranger and you did not invite me in, I needed clothes and you did not clothe me, I was sick and in prison and you did not look after me.'

44 "They also will answer, 'Lord, when did we see you hungry or thirsty or a stranger or needing clothes or sick or in prison, and did not help you?'

45 "He will reply, 'Truly I tell you, whatever you did not do for one of the least of these, you did not do for me.'

46 "Then they will go away to eternal punishment, but the righteous to eternal life."

So, what's this story saying to US, here and now?

Jules Fine is based on a real person and that is his real name. He was a great mentor to Mike as he progressed through the advertising business.

Of Jewish extraction and an emigrant to the USA from central Europe in the post-war years, he never got to start and run his own business, so Fine Communications is an invention. But he did get to become Vice Chairman and Strategic Director of a major global ad agency.

Jules was a humble and sensitive man of great wisdom and strong values, and we think he'd appreciate the role and actions we've created for him here.

In this parable, we see Jesus using a teaching style that has real edge.

Once again, there is only black and white, with a dash of hyperbole for good measure. We've seen it elsewhere. In an oral teaching tradition, Jesus was extremely keen to make sure he got his point across.

This time we've chosen not to dumb that down or introduce any shades of grey.

When we sign up to something: a cause, team, or belief, we then have a choice.

Do we subscribe in words alone as armchair supporters?

Or do we subscribe in words and actions and become an active fan base?

In modern parlance: do we choose to talk the talk or walk the walk?

Jesus is clear. Our Christian faith should permeate our whole life and influence our values, our words, and, crucially, our actions.

If you want to understand more about this, read the book of James. He was Jesus' brother and was just as black and white:

'What good is it, my brothers and sisters, if someone claims to have faith but has no deeds? Can such faith save them?... As the body without the spirit is dead, so faith without deeds is dead ' (James 2: 14 & 26).

Clearly, the way we work out our faith in our lives is for each of us to discern and decide. Not all Christians are called to the ministry or to overseas mission. Some are called to work out their faith in sports, business, entertainment, teaching, parenting, and volunteering. Some in education and others even in advertising!

The question Jesus is asking each one of us here is, whatever it is we do for a living, whether we are willing to allow our life to become a witness to him: "Where do *you* stand?"

Reflection and prayer | Am I walking the walk?

· ·

_____

_____

_____

_____

_____

_____

What's this story saying to me, here and now?

· ·

_____

_____

_____

_____

_____

_____

_____

If you have been reading the parables sequentially, you've now reached the end.

You have traveled with Jesus through his ministry and heard his teaching as he told it then and as he might have told it today.

You may have preferred the original versions to the rewirings. That's ok. We prefer many of them ourselves! All of our rewirings are written with the intent that you'll read Jesus' words afresh. It's all about him.

But we believe it is important to keep Jesus' teaching relevant and contemporary, and we hope we have helped in that respect.

Some scholars have hailed the parables as the greatest ever teaching.

Others have dismissed them as being too contrived, too simplistic, or irrelevant to life today.

What do *you* think?

Where do *you* stand?

Afterword

Jesus told his parables to a wide range of audiences and for a variety of purposes.

He told them to his small band of disciples to encourage and train them; to vast crowds to inform and inspire them; as guidance to those genuinely seeking enlightenment; to hostile groups such as the Pharisees to chastise them; and as a riposte to scheming opponents and their efforts to discredit or entrap him.

As we've been writing this book, we've found ourselves thinking time and again about the effect the parables would have had on these varying audiences.

Would they have been intrigued? Challenged? Shocked? Encouraged? Stunned? Confused? Informed? Bewildered? Enlightened? Annoyed? Enthused? Angered? Affirmed?

All of the above.

What they would not have been is bored or disinterested.

Our aim has been to help people of today experience those parables afresh, whether hearing them for the first time or the umpteenth.

We hope that, as you've read them, you've tried to stand in the shoes of those various audiences, to project yourself into their mindsets, and that you've also tried to visualize Jesus, with all his human passion and spiritual power, standing in front of you, talking directly to you.

If not, go back and read some of them again, not our "rewirings," but the originals, as Jesus told them. That's why we've included them.

As with all scripture, we should expect the parables to speak to us today. We hope that in our commentaries, we've touched on some ways in which they do this.

Clearly, we do not know all of you readers individually and personally. So, we haven't been able to tailor our messages to each and every one of you. But Jesus does know you, intimately. And if you give him the time and space to do so, he will tell you precisely what these parables mean for you.

Finally, Jesus told his parable stories so they could be shared with and retold to others, particularly to those who couldn't or wouldn't come and hear them from him firsthand.

So, if you know someone who doesn't yet know Jesus, and they are someone who you feel Jesus wants to speak with, please share this book with them so he can do so!

May the grace of our Lord Jesus Christ, the love of God, and the fellowship of the Holy Spirit be with you all (2 Corinthians 13:14) now and for evermore. Amen.

Mike, Ivan and Jason

· ·

Biographies

Mike Elms has more than 40 years' experience in business, marketing and advertising. As UK CEO of two major ad agencies, Ogilvy & Mather and Tempus Group plc, he has worked with a wide range of blue-chip companies at C-Suite level, including: Unilever, Nestle, Ford, Mercedes, Chrysler, DHL, Shell and Guinness. He has also advised a wide range of Christian organizations. An experienced church leader and preacher, he is Board Chair of Lògòs Foundation, a Christian charity focused on using advertising and PR to advance the Gospel.

Ivan Filby is the President and CEO of Seedbed, a subsidiary of Asbury Theological Seminary. He has had a distinguished career in higher education and has a Ph.D. in Management and an MA in Evangelism. He taught at The University of Dublin: Trinity College for sixteen years before moving to the USA to chair the Management Department at Greenville University. He is the author of *Livestream: Learning to Minister in the Power of the Holy Spirit* and *Speak Tenderly: Prophetic Ministry Seasoned with Grace.*

Jason Moore has created the original artwork for *Jesus Unbranded* using his unique skill to combine the use of AI with his own artistic sensibilities.

Inside Mike's mind: 'Unbranding Jesus'

During my time as an adman I've encountered a whole bunch of brands that have lost their way and strayed from their original purpose or mission.

A succession of marketing regimes may have added, subtracted, or, in a variety of ways, 'tinkered' with the product or service itself.

A succession of advertising executives may have tried to make their mark by putting their own stamp and 'spin' on the brand messaging.

And so the brand ends up in a very different place from which it started.

Over the years I have discovered that the only remedy is to strip all that 'baggage' away and go back to the brand's roots. To rediscover the original purpose and proposition that made it great in the first place. To see, understand, and respect the original, authentic brand. And then allow it to speak for itself again.

I've given that stripping away process a label. I call it 'unbranding.'

Over the centuries Jesus has been constantly interpreted and reinterpreted. Some things have been added, others lost.

Some people and organizations have sought to hijack Christianity, and even Jesus himself, to use them to serve their own agenda. For reasons good and bad. Let me stress, I'm simply observing here, not judging.

As Ivan and I pursued our Mission of 'Keeping the stories alive', we realized something deeper was occurring. We found ourselves standing among his audience, hearing him speak directly to us. We listened intently to every parable he told. And by placing them in chronological order, we got to travel with him throughout the whole of his ministry.

Through the lens of the stories he told, we came face to face with the original, authentic, unadulterated Jesus.

Such is the power of the parables.

So our mission became to let them speak for themselves again.

As you immerse yourself in them, our prayer is that you too will find yourself standing in the awesome presence of the original, authentic and 'unbranded' Jesus; and that you will hear him speaking directly to you, here and now.

Mike

· ·

Inside Ivan's mind: 'Writing in the Spirit'

Any author will tell you that a blank sheet of paper is a very intimidating thing indeed.

Only your creativity can put ink on paper; writer's block is always lurking just around the corner.

But once pen is put to paper, the creative juices begin to flow.

Mike and I discovered that being presented with many sheets of paper full of the words of Jesus, together with a divine instruction to re-imagine them, is *infinitely more intimidating.*

Who were we to even contemplate that?

But once we made a start we discovered that time after time, story after story, the Holy Spirit was inspiring us.

Many a time we looked at each other after a completed rewiring and asked: 'where on earth did that come from?'

The answer was, of course, nowhere on earth.

Mike does not have a degree in theology. But he does have a passionate and abiding love of Jesus. As an ordained minister I was happy to become the mind to his heart, and together, I believe we made a pretty good team.

Our aim was to ensure our theology was sound but not 'in-your-face'. So, we avoided terms such as Sanctification, Incarnation, Absolution and even Salvation. But whilst the words may not be there, the concepts they encapsulate most definitely are. Because they are baked into the parables.

Rewiring the storylines was only the half of it, though.

We then had to discern what each parable is saying to us, here and now.

Again we sought to strike a balance between theology and readability.

What is the eternal, spiritual theme that each of these every day, worldly storylines has embedded within it? There too the Spirit inspired us. What we have written was his message to us.

But he may, no make that *almost certainly will*, have a different message for each of you.

We urge you to let him inspire you also. As you hear Jesus speaking to you through his parables—our words or his own—ask the Spirit to reveal what the words have to say to you, here and now.

And if the Spirit gives you another storyline, don't be afraid to grab a blank piece of paper and start writing!

Ivan

. . . .

Inside Jason's mind: 'Seeing is believing'

AI, Artificial Intelligence, is a topic that stirs emotions.

Some see it as a bright new future: a huge opportunity for the world.

Others as a dark menace: an existential threat to mankind.

As always, reality lies somewhere between these two extremes.

Mike and Ivan observed to me that if we had named it for what it actually is—Automated Information—it would be a whole lot less scary.

I liked that.

(They are also very keen to emphasise that the only AI involved in rewiring the parables was Authors' Insights powered by Amazing Imaginations!)

Let's be clear. AI is a tool. But tools can be used for good or for evil. A screwdriver is a tool. It can be used to put up a shelf or construct a bomb. A Kalashnikov AK47 is also a tool. It can be used to maintain law and order or commit acts of terrorism.

AI can be used for either good or evil. As can music, literature, photography and so on.

Speaking personally, I use it in a design and illustration context and I like to think I wear a white hat!

I use AI as the starting point: it helps me to begin to bring a concept to life.

But I have to then input my own artistic and design skills. And use other techy tools to get the concept to look just the way I want it to look. No, let me rephrase that: to get the concept the way Mike and Ivan want it to look.

Their minds, guided by the Spirit, have created a fresh vision, a verbal picture, for each of the parables. My job has been to understand that vision and bring it to reality by turning it into an arresting image.

And there you have another way of expressing AI: Arresting Images.

Arresting Images powered by Artistic Inspiration.

In Jesus' day, stories were told in words, to be retold and handed down, generation to generation.

In our day, we are more visually attuned. If Jesus were telling the parables now, he'd almost certainly have some visual aids.

Because, these days, a single, striking image is worth a thousand words.

But please—don't tell Mike and Ivan!

Jason